INSTRUMENTS OF DEATH

An exhilarating symphony began as mortars, machine guns, grenades, rockets, and assault rifles played their deadly theme, repeated by echoes from the surrounding hills. The music was glorious. At times it almost burst the eardrums with a wall of pure sound. At other times each weapon's unique noise signature could be distinguished, as rifle and rocket played point and counterpoint. It was Beethoven's Fifth Symphony, Tchaikovsky's 1812 Overture, and every martial theme that ever raced through the frenetic mind of Richard Wagner, and it was all synthesized and mechanized, played by instruments of death. Its effect on me was almost sublime. For the first time in my life I could understand Patton, Napoleon, and other war-lovers. For the moment, at least, there was no greater glory than what I was experiencing.

Below me the Sandinistas were dying.

SOLDIER
WITHOUT
FORTUNE

Dr. John L. McClure

A DELL BOOK

Published by
Dell Publishing Co., Inc.
1 Dag Hammarskjold Plaza
New York, New York 10017

This book is respectfully dedicated to the memory of Rick, Aguila, Pedro, and the others who, in various countries, have become part of the jungle.

Every event and every person in this narrative is true. Some names have been changed to protect operatives still working on covert missions—sanctioned and free-lance.

Printed in the United States of America

December 1987

10 9 8 7 6 5 4 3 2 1

KRI

I was alone.

Alone in the Nicaraguan jungle with five hundred rounds of ammunition, a Belgian FN FAL assault rifle, my trusty old Colt .45 pistol, two daggers, and three hand grenades. Alone, except for the eight thousand Sandinista soldiers in this zone of the Nicaraguan civil war.

Eden Pastora Gomez, "Commander Zero" of the democratic forces battling the Sandinista government, had ordered Camp Z-3 abandoned. We had received word from collaborators that the Costa Rican security forces were going to raid this camp, which straddled the Rio San Juan, the border between the two countries. Communication equipment, antennas, weapons, and men were to be transferred twenty kilometers up the river to Camp Tango, our largest base in the southern front of Nicaragua.

Pastora and his dozen handpicked bodyguards had left for the interior of Costa Rica in an attempt to liberate a shipment of machine guns, mortars, and medical supplies confiscated by Costa Rican authorities. My orders were to supervise the transfer of men and equipment, to remain at Z-3 after their departure, and await further orders from Pastora, which would be relayed to me through Tango.

As dusk settled a raucous flock of jungle birds lit in the trees at the edge of the camp. Dragonflies swarmed after the mosquitoes that rose like mist from the fetid jungle. When the sated dragonflies quit swooping in dog-fighter flight, bats came out for their turn at the mosquitoes.

It was soon night.

Howler monkeys, locally called *kongos*, roared like leopards on their night sweep beyond the perimeter. I have never gotten used to the sound. The howler is said to be one of the loudest creatures in the world. I can believe that. I woke sweating at 0400 hours to the fearsome noise of their dawn patrol.

Like New York gangs kicking over garbage cans on their turf, the monkeys mark their boundaries morning and night by terrifying the rest of the jungle. I didn't need it; I was already scared. Pastora had left me there two days before. I had slept in my camouflage fatigues, pistol belt, and harness, loosening my grip on the FAL just long enough to spray my sunburned skin with insect repellent. It stung like hell. For two long nights and days I had waited for the escort promised by Pastora. The cries of the *kongo* troop seemed louder this night and their fearsome screams weren't helping my nerves.

Maybe they had been startled by a Sandinista patrol looking for Pastora's only gringo staff member. They had barely missed me—a bullet clipped hair from my arm—in an ambush a few days before. There could be a company within a quarter mile and I wouldn't hear them. A battalion could be in the acre of jungle surrounding me and I wouldn't see them.

If the Sandinistas came, I would die. I could fight them to the death, shoot myself to avoid capture, or jump into the river, trying to avoid the river's freshwater man-eating sharks, and try to swim across the Rio to safety in Costa Rica. I figured I'd shoot myself.

That was such a bad joke, it calmed me. I began to remember who I was and what I was doing. I quit reacting.

I sat, propped my rifle against the building, loosened my pistol belt, and leaned back against the wall. I peered into the darkness and began to think about how I came to be sitting on the bank of this jungle river in Central America, heavily armed and wearing the uniform and insignia of a Nicaraguan Contra.

CHAPTER ONE

MARIEL

Military service is and has been a tradition in my family. From the seventeenth century members of my clan have been soldiers and scholars who came to the New World from the Isle of Man. Every adult male in the family had seen combat service in some theater of World War II. It was, I suppose, natural that my twelfth and thirteenth years were spent at a military academy on the west coast of Florida. The school had a heavy Latin attendance, sons of the military elite of Cuba, Venezuela, Colombia, and Panama. One of my roommates and close friends was a young Cuban named Miguel, the son of a prominent Havana engineer.

It was during our time at the academy when Fulgencio Batista once again seized power in Cuba by a coup d'état. The Cuban boys were ecstatic. Corked green bottles of dark aromatic liquor appeared from footlockers where they had lain rolled in sweatshirts. Miguel's rattan-wrapped jug passed from room to room, up and down our floor. I had my first drink of rum from it. And from that hot night in 1952 the dusky-sweet rum taste of Caribbean adventure, political intrigue, and the headiness of revolution was in my blood.

Maybe that taste had something to do with my first career choice. Shortly before my sixteenth birthday, I lied about my age and joined the United States Marine Corps. Boot camp at Parris Island was followed by two years in a special infantry unit. But Marine infantry didn't jump out of airplanes, and that's what my favorite stepfather had done. My memories of him had faded after his death, but sharp images of spit-shined jump boots and the silver wings of a paratrooper remained. So I left the Marines at the end of my hitch and joined the Army's famed 82nd Airborne Division. I finished one hitch in the paratroops and dabbled in a variety of civilian work. But one morning I picked up a newspaper and found the name of an old barracks buddy in a casualty list. I volunteered for Vietnam.

But over the years the dormitory party for Batista still came back in my daydreams. Meanwhile, a few years earlier, another Cuban had seized power in the Pearl of the Antilles. Only this takeover had not been followed by the same celebrations. Quite the contrary.

Miami, in particular, was inundated with Cubans who had fled Fidel Castro's new regime. In the first few years ten percent of the island's population had left to begin a new life in the United States. They abandoned their homeland rather than submit to Communist tyranny. These new arrivals rapidly began rebuilding their lives, despite the antipathy of some South Florida residents, and many achieved economic and professional success in South Florida within a few years.

However, in 1980, in a master stroke, Fidel Castro announced that the port of Mariel on the northern shore of Cuba would be declared open. The discontented would be free to leave. The Carter Administration was caught flat-footed and, as they fumbled for a response, hundreds and later thousands of Cuban-Americans raced toward Mariel aboard anything that would float. They were frantic to locate relatives and friends and bring them to America.

Many of these Cuban-Americans were cheated by boat captains eager to make a quick buck and were charged exorbitant fees—as much as fifteen hundred dollars per refugee passenger—by these greedy parasites.

Once the Freedom Flotilla—as it came to be called—arrived at Mariel they learned that, like many deals that seem too good to be true, this one had a catch. For every friend or relative one wished to take from Mariel, Fidel Castro put at least two criminals, prostitutes, or mental patients on the boat. People who balked at this were threatened at gunpoint. In a few cases Cuban-Americans were actually detained by Communist authorities.

In all over one hundred thousand refugees departed Mariel for Florida's shores.

After my last service tour I had tried my hand

at programming computers while I went to college at night on the GI Bill. But the behavioral
sciences interested me and, after earning a BA in
psychology, I went on to graduate school.

I completed a doctoral program in clinical psychology and was serving an internship at a South
Florida mental-health clinic near the docks where
the refugees arrived daily. Cuban psychiatrists
were kind enough to provide each of the recently
released patients with a list of medications they
had been receiving in the Cuban hospitals and
asylums. When U.S. Marines assigned to the re-
ception station at the Truman Annex of the Key
West, Florida, naval base brought refugees with
obvious mental problems to the clinic, those refugees would happily present us with their lists of
psychotropic medications.

One of my duties at this clinic was administration of the Florida State Indigent Drug Program.
During the Mariel boatlift much of my job consisted of simply filling prescriptions written by
Cuban doctors. I had neither time nor facilities to
make my own diagnoses, and some of these people were coming unglued as I talked to them.
Trained in behavior therapy, about all I could do
was translate their prescriptions and feed the de-
pendencies begun by doctors in the employ of the
Cuban state.

Later I saw many of these unfortunates in therapy and when the police brought them to the
emergency room at Florida Keys Memorial Hospital. One of my first and saddest cases involved a
fourteen-year-old boy. His father had fled Cuba

without his family twelve years before. The father had jumped at the chance to be reunited with his family. He had sailed from Key West to Mariel in a nineteen-foot fishing boot to retrieve his wife and children.

The boy was catatonic when they arrived in Florida.

The stress of being uprooted and subjected to a rigorous ninety-mile trip in a small, open boat had proved too much for him. When a wave washed over the craft the boy went into an apparent state of shock from which, several weeks later when I saw him, he had not yet emerged.

The father was beside himself. Years of guilt were amplified by the boy's retreat into a safe and private world where he could be hurt no more.

Another sixteen-year-old boy—again with a distraught, guilt-ridden father—was brought to my office by the police. This boy looked about ten, because his growth had been stunted by severe malnutrition during the crucial formative years. Another member of the family told me that for two years in Cuba they had nothing to eat but rice and eggs. This teenager had worse problems, though, than the physical ones that were so apparent. He had been prostituted to homosexuals in Cuba so that the family might eat better.

This boy was brought in by the police because he had been found sexually molesting his eighteen-month-old half brother.

A young Cuban-American lady had chartered a fishing boat from one of the local docks and gone to Mariel to retrieve her mother. She was able to

bring her mother back—as long as she took four
whores shoved into her craft by Cuban police.
The lady's mother, unfortunately, was one of
those who had been escorted to the clinic by Marines. She clutched her prescription tightly and
demanded her *diazepano*, better known to us in
the United States by the brand name of Valium.
The lady was not seriously mentally ill, but what
I termed a garden-variety neurotic. However, the
years of living in a socialist society had made her
a creature dependent on institutional support.
Rather than work, she sat in her daughter's house
incredulously complaining about the U.S. government's unwillingness to support her.

During my years of graduate school I had
worked as a counselor at a state prison. I had
observed the same clinging dependency exhibited
by veteran convicts that I saw in this poor Cuban
dama.

The younger lady was beside herself. "I hate to
admit it, but I wish I had never gone to Mariel,"
she told me tearfully.

Even though this was my internship year and I
had considerably more on my mind than the
problems of the Marielitos, as they came to be
called in South Florida, the effect of communism
on these poor people made a profound impression
on me.

What kind of society, I thought, would have its
citizens prostituting their children to male homosexuals in order to eat? What kind of society
would turn basically normal human beings into

clinging, neurotic-dependent types who were always asking that things be done for them?

At this time also, in South Florida, another effect of the Mariel boatlift was being felt in the growing crime rate and the especially heinous crimes determined to have been committed by Marielitos. Fidel Castro had sent the scum of his jails into America, mixed in with the legitimate refugees. The Dade County medical examiner was quoted in the Miami *Herald* as saying that they committed the most horrible atrocities on their victims that he had ever witnessed. And Cuban-American mental-health professionals with whom I consulted told me they were horrified at the sadomasochistic element they had been observing among the Mariel homosexuals.

Finally, my internship year dragged to a merciful end. I moved back to the mainland and began a private practice, supplementing my income by resuming a part-time assistant professorship at a nearby state university. With the economic security the teaching job provided, I was able to wholeheartedly, yet comfortably, build what soon became a thriving practice. Not only did I see patients, but I often worked in courtrooms for both defense and prosecution attorneys, giving expert testimony on the mental status of criminal defendants.

But years in the military and a life spent knocking about had given me a vision of the world and its realities that was quite different from the majority of my laboratory-bound, solely classroom-educated colleagues in psychology.

The money was good and helping people had intrinsic rewards, but I found no camaraderie with other psychologists, as I had found with military men and other hard-living types.

Psychology could not give me a lifetime of satisfaction, so after a couple of years I started thinking about another career.

But meanwhile my practice was lucrative and I had indulged myself by buying something I had wanted for a long time. A new Corvette. It turned out to have been a fateful decision.

Believe it or not, there was a practical component in my choice of cars. One night I was escorting my last patient out to her car. She noticed that I was getting into a beat-up old Camaro.

"Too bad you can't afford a decent car, Doctor."

CHAPTER TWO

FREEDOM

People like to see signs of success and prosperity in their doctor, especially when they're paying him eighty-five dollars an hour. The Corvette was a symbol of my success. And in some cases the Corvette led to my patients' increased expectation that they would rapidly solve their problems in therapy with such an obviously successful doctor.

Meanwhile, however, psychology was not giving me the challenge or satisfaction I had anticipated and I was casting about for another profession. Since I had spent almost nine years in both reserve and active military service, I began thinking in terms of a military venture.

I even considered going back on active duty, especially when I was told that with my Ph.D. I would be automatically promoted to captain. However, my age and memories of having to toe the line for a few martinets and desk-bound administrators discouraged me from returning to active duty in the armed forces of the United States of America.

I found myself attending gun shows and putting in hours on the range with my newly acquired AR-15 assault rifle. My wife noticed *Soldier of Fortune* lying around the house, a magazine she hadn't seen me buy before. My psychologist colleagues considered the magazine prima facie evidence of a schizoid personality disorder, while my drinking buddies—mostly law-enforcement officers—were avid readers of the sometimes disjointed "there I was, surrounded by Vietcong" stories but were more interested in the astute technical articles about the latest in military armament.

I began reading more and more about Central America, especially Nicaragua, where Jimmy Carter had facilitated the Sandinista victory in 1979 by his withdrawal of aid to the government of General Anastasio Somoza.

I read of the exploits of Eden Pastora Gomez, the famous Commander Zero, who appeared to be on his way to becoming a legend. His handsome face had been on front pages all over the world when he had led a raid in which the entire Congress of Nicaragua was held hostage during the war against the Somoza regime.

When he broke with the Sandinista government after this war, he reappeared on the front pages, again as a rebel leader. He seemed colorful and daring. I thought a visit to Central America and perhaps a meeting with this dashing commander might prove interesting.

This happened sooner than I thought.

My Corvette was one kind of symbol to me, and another kind to a former employer. She was, it seems, intensely jealous of my overnight success in the practice of psychology. She started a rumor that made its way to the state licensing board: I could afford an expensive car so soon after entry into private practice because my true profession was selling cocaine. To add a little spice to the story she even claimed that I had sex with my female patients.

I was not a cocaine dealer, nor was I having sex with my patients. I demanded an investigation. I had always tried to live by the famous maxims of the late Nelson Algren, author of *Man With the Golden Arm* and *A Walk On the Wild Side:* Never eat at a place called "Mom's"; never play cards with a man named "Doc"; and, most important, never go to bed with a woman whose troubles are greater than your own. Not only did my female patients have greater problems than I, but the ethical standards I had been trained to observe in my doctoral program were even more strict than those of the American Psychological Association.

When the state investigators learned that there was no truth to the allegation, my former employer left Florida in disgrace and I closed my practice of psychology in disgust. I walked out of my plush fifteen-hundred-dollar-a-month office, leaving behind the furniture, the volumes in their bookcases, and the diplomas hanging on the wall.

I never looked back.

When I made the decision definitely to leave

the practice of psychology, I put the word out among acquaintances that I was available for paramilitary operations. Being a native, I'd grown up with locals who were now in fairly high positions on both sides of the law in South Florida. It wasn't long before I received a contract for an operation.

I told my wife that I was going mountain climbing in Mexico with a couple of old army buddies.

Actually, they were outlaw bikers I'd known since we were kids and we really went there to collect a debt owed a South Florida cocaine dealer by a lawyer who had skipped the country. The lawyer thought he was safe behind his bodyguard of Mexican speed freaks, but he hadn't paid the local *jefe de policia* nearly enough to deserve his friendship and protection.

We did.

My biker buddies had gone to the Florida Industrial School for Boys about the time I went to Parris Island, and their military experience consisted entirely of the hours they had spent watching John Wayne movies while serving their sentences. Our assault technique was not to be found in any military manual. We had agreed to try to get into the villa by pretending to be drunken *turistas* who had mistaken the place for a brothel, but as soon as the gate was cracked one of my burly companions pulled the pin on an old Mark II fragmentation grenade, which had probably spent the last twenty years sitting in a Florida

National Guard armory, and flung it at the surprised guard.

The grenade hit the gate and bounced back toward us! I got most of my body around the corner, but managed to catch a piece of the frag with my right kneecap. But the explosion and our yelling charge through the dust with drawn pistols scared hell out of the Mexicans. The white-faced lawyer we had gone after was screaming gibberish at us, in a state of shock, as he handed over a heavy Haliburton suitcase. "Crude but effective" was the way I characterized the mission.

My wound wasn't all that bad to begin with, but Mexican hospitals' sterile technique being what it is, I came home with a severe bone infection. But a lot of cash in small U.S. bills helped me bear the pain, although I vowed never to go on such a bullshit operation with assholes as team members.

A few weeks later my wife came home from nursing school to find me packing camouflage fatigues and combat boots into a duffel bag.

"What's going on?" she demanded, hands on hips.

"I'm going to war in Nicaragua," I replied, without looking up from my task.

"You're going to do what?"

"Don't scream, damnit."

"Why not? What else should I do? It doesn't look like I can stop you . . . and how was I supposed to know this was going to happen?" Tears were welling in her dark eyes.

"You know I haven't been happy in psychology. And since that bitch slandered me I'm just sick of the whole snake pit. I don't care if Johnny wets the bed or if Henry and Louise get a divorce. I don't even care if that schizophrenic kid goes to the electric chair for killing his father. I've had it!"

"And you didn't think you owed me an explanation?"

"I tried to tell you," I said, finally raising up from the pile of olive-drab gear. "But I was too angry to deal with this on a verbal level. The message was there for you though—you've seen the magazines I've been reading. And what did you think when you woke up in the middle of the night and found me sitting in the dark, cleaning my guns?"

"I thought you'd gone crazy." She nearly spat out the cigarette she was trying to light. "What are you going to do? Walk out on nine years of college, your practice, on our life . . . on me?"

"On the nine years—yes. On the practice— hell, yes. On you and our life—never," I said, reaching out to touch her with what I hoped was a reassuring pat. "Here's the game plan. I'm going south to check out the Sandinistas."

"And why are you going to do that?" She withdrew slightly from my touch.

"U.S. newspapers aren't printing anything but releases from the press agents of the competitive factions. I'm well educated on the region, and even I don't know what's going on down there. But I do know it's important, not only to American interests, but to the survival of democracy in

Latin America. If the Sandinistas are basically a decent bunch that are getting a raw deal from the American press and government, I'll offer my services to them. If they are Communists, I'll go on to Costa Rica, find this guy Pastora, and join his forces. If they don't need advisers, hell, I'll sign on as a grunt."

"What is the future in all this?" No matter how hysterical, Alexandra always retained a ruthless grip on reality.

"Either way there's opportunity," I replied. "If I hook up with the Sandinistas or Pastora's group, my goal is going to be the formation of a private security company that can handle clandestine work for free-world governments. With my psychological training and experience, I can handle screening and interrogation, and with what I learned in the military, I can do everything from individual combat through training troops and even running operations. Uncle Sam taught me superbly."

"Well, be careful down there and don't fall off a mountain like you did in Mexico." Alexandra could not always be counted on for unconditional support.

"Look, good things will come from all this, Alex," I said, pacing as if I was back in the classroom, lecturing. "I'll live and fight with the side I choose. I won't need to take pay; trust is all I'll want . . . at first. But I'll let them know up front I want a contract to provide security services after the war. Hell, I might even get in on some CIA operation."

"What will I do? Sit and wait to hear you're dead?" She still hadn't managed to light her cigarette.

"No. Why don't you sell the cars and all this crap?" I waved at our suburban home. "And come down to Central America once I have a place set up for you? Meanwhile, I've put away enough money for you to live on while I do what I have to do."

"But you don't have to do anything." Angry tears sprang to her eyes. "Why can't you be a psychologist?"

"Fuck psychology! B. F. Skinner can make rats and pigeons tap-dance and whistle 'Dixie.' But a century after Wertheimer and a billion dollars after Freud, about all psychology has managed to do is teach retarded kids to tie their shoelaces in two years instead of three. As for clinical psychology . . . well, you know the patients I see—psychotics that can't get better, neurotics that won't get better, and the character disorders that are in therapy looking for excuses to avoid responsibility for having fucked up their lives.

"All I can do is counsel people who are basically normal—but have a few problems in living—to take charge of their own lives. What I do for them is nothing more than they could do all by themselves with a little common sense and motivation. I'm sick of listening to the problems of people who don't have any."

"But that's what you do so well, John—you motivate people."

"Fuck them if they can't motivate themselves," I barked.

"What about your work for the courts? You love that."

"Sure, I love showing inkblots to dirtbags and trying to figure out why they like to rape and kill," I sneered. "Granted, I *do* love matching wits with the lawyers—especially when they're paying for it. But I don't make a net contribution to justice. All I'm really doing is selling jargon on the witness stand for a hundred and twenty-five dollars an hour.

"Look, honey, you're almost through with nursing school. Finish up and by then I'll have a comfortable place for you down there. But if you can't handle this, or don't want to handle it, get a divorce."

"I don't want a divorce," she pouted. "You're not getting rid of me that easily . . . dammit, I like being married to a doctor."

"I'm sorry, Alex, but when that bitch laid on those bullshit accusations, not one damned voice was raised in my defense. I took a good look at my so-called colleagues and didn't like what I saw.

"In school, it was different. Remember how warm my professors were?" She nodded in agreement. "Private practitioners aren't like academics. For the most part, they're greedy, jealous wimps. Christ, you remember the APA convention. The folks I had the best time with and learned the most from in the seminars were the radical feminists. Hell, most of them are lesbians, but they're more macho than half of the so-called men in this profession. I'm not doing anything important here, and there's a world in trouble out there.

"Alex, help me pack. Fuck psychology! I'm going to Central America!"

CHAPTER THREE

CENTRAL AMERICA
101

I booked a flight to Managua, the capital of
Nicaragua, by way of El Salvador. On a hot July
day in 1983 I flew from Miami International Airport to the incredibly beautiful city of San Salvador.

Waiting in the airport lounge for my connecting flight to Managua, I stood by a large window
overlooking the runways, sipped a rum and Coke
—free to passengers in the transit lounge—and
watched the incoming and departing flights.

I was joined at my observation post by a large,
pleasant-looking man in a white linen suit with an
off-white silk handkerchief protruding jauntily
from its pocket. As we watched a jet landed bearing the logo of Aeronica, the state-run airline of
Nicaragua.

"Here come the bad boys," my companion remarked.

I grunted something affirmative and noticed
that he appeared to be sizing me up. Being a Flo-
ridian, I was darkly tanned, and—even though I

was in my forties—lean and hard from daily workouts in the *do jang* of Dr. Ji Sung Song, a Korean *Tae Kwon Do* grand master. I wore a khaki safari suit and had my hair cropped close, GI style, and no doubt presented a somewhat military appearance. When I ordered a fresh drink in passable Spanish, I think my visitor got the impression that I was an old Central American hand on some mysterious business in El Salvador.

"Lovely country, El Salvador. Have you been here before?"

Such cultivated, knowing courtesy. All he needed was a fez or a Panama hat and he could have been Sydney Greenstreet's bigger, harder younger brother.

"No," I muttered across the top of my drink. It was time for me to be strong and silent. He looked important. Every stitch of his Palm Beach suit said "power." I wanted him to know I was somebody who knew how to act around people like him.

"All of El Salvador is as beautiful as that skyline. Sometimes you can't see it, because they burn their fields off after the harvest. But the industry of the Salvadorenos is part of the beauty of the country.

"El Salvador is troubled, but the people work, and they have faith. The Church is strong, and the government was just returned to office by a landslide."

"That's not what we're getting in the news at home."

"Ah, of course not, but that is because the

status quo is never remarkable. Free-press news-men invariably assume that the work of reportage is to show their audience things they cannot read in an encyclopedia. That's why they call it 'news.'" A tremor shook his square, bulky shoul-ders as he chuckled amiably at his own joke. The exhaust of a jet taking off sympathetically wrin-kled the mountains and bulged the quivering plate glass toward me.

"As an example," he continued to lecture. "Adventurous reporters were taken on tours of guerrilla camps—two were even killed. The more cautious were guided through the streets of San Salvador by guerrilla representatives and shown the bodies remaining from drunken *campesino* ar-guments of the previous night—one harsh word and the rest of a dispute down here is settled with the ubiquitous machete. These corpses were pre-sented as indisputable evidence of rabid right-wing death squads.

"When the elections came reporters were so jaded by sensational sight-seeing expeditions, they were not interested in the fact that the aver-age Salvadorean—eighty percent, in fact—braved guerrilla gunfire to vote. Nor could the reporters believe that ninety percent of that number voted to return the incumbents to office. You see, newsmen's vision is colored by their hun-ger for new things, not a hunger for understand-ing."

"Yes, but couldn't the government conduct a few tours of their own?"

"Theoretically the government could, but they

would not, and the press would not believe them. Traditional, strong-state conservative governments never manage the press well because they do not recognize any need to explain themselves to rumormongers. American reporters would not believe them because they reflexively believe any government has something to hide."

"You're pretty damn pessimistic for somebody with your apparent connections and interests." He was beginning to irritate me, simply because he was so self-possessed, and so sure I wanted to listen. Of course the fact that I did want to listen didn't help.

"No, not at all, my friend." He looked straight at me and smiled. His blue-eyed, square, pale face was open, strong, and intelligent. "El Salvador's future is, I assure you, quite rosy. In the coming presidential elections the left will attack the right, thinking the moderate Socialists to be their friends. Those Socialists, however, are largely Salvadoran Nationalists, and they are well-enough connected with the left to know that the guerrillas want El Salvador to be another Cuban province. Even D'Aubisson, the leader of El Salvador's right wing, already knows Duarte will win because his CIA contacts have told him so. Furthermore, D'Aubisson knows his victory in the presidential elections would leave El Salvador a Central American Rhodesia, with himself in the part of Ian Smith. And D'Aubisson has no desire to watch his country burn until he is forced to supervise the transfer of power to the guerrillas.

"No. Duarte shall win, D'Aubisson shall be

happy with the outcome because he is a patriot, and the United States of America shall continue to halfheartedly supply the Army since the press will be convinced that 'death squads' will not run the country."

"What's happening in Guatemala?" I asked.

"Well," he replied, "General Rios-Montt has pretty much taken care of the Communist threat with his civil defense program. Remember, down here civil defense does not mean running into air-raid shelters. It means groups of civilians who very actively defend themselves from Communist insurgents. The Guatemalan Army went into the hills with a program which not only gave the peasants rice, beans, and seed to plant, it also gave them weapons and a bit of training so that they could defend themselves and not have to rely on a heavy army presence. And the plan worked. When the Communist guerrillas would come into the villages they found little in the way of fertile soil for their type of seed. The people were well fed, well armed, and had a stake in their own future.

"However," he went on. "I don't expect Rios-Montt to be around much longer. He's a 'born-again' Protestant in a Catholic country and just a bit too heavy-handed at times, especially for your State Department friends in Washington," he added.

"Where do the guerrillas come from?" I asked. "Nicaragua?"

"Well, they are trained, of course, in Cuba and

Mexico and their arms are funneled into Guatemala, courtesy of the Sandinistas."

I said, "So, the Sandinistas really are Marxists."

He snorted. "What else? In fact," he said, "as far back as 1975, Sandinistas were meeting Russian submarines off the Pacific coast of Nicaragua to pick up suitcases full of American twenty-dollar bills with which to finance their war against Somoza. Not only are they Marxists, they are the bully boys of Central America."

"Look around you," he said, gesturing expansively at the verdant hills in the background. "This is a beautiful country; these are solid people; this is an area rich in natural resources that should be developed through a combination of free enterprise and government initiative. But as long as the Sandinistas keep fanning the flames of insurgency in nearby countries, there can't be the peace necessary for a good business and development climate.

"Where are you headed from here?" he asked.

"Managua."

A conspiratorial leer appeared on his face and he nudged me in the ribs with a thick elbow. "Well, I don't envy you. You had better keep a low profile. What's your cover?" At this point I realized that my companion—if not in the business himself—certainly thought that I was an intelligence agent.

"I'm an insurance broker," he chuckled. He presented me with his card, which bore a Toronto address. Not wanting to appear as naive as I really was, I didn't ask him what a Canadian insurance broker was doing in the middle of war-torn Central America.

I extracted a card from my wallet and handed it to him.

"A psychologist," he chortled. "Excellent, m'boy, excellent. Latins respect titles. Hmm, yes," he mused.

"Borge is the one to watch out for in Nicaragua. He's the Minister of the Interior and, of course, all the police come under his jurisdiction. Ortega is the public head of the junta, but Borge is the one with Soviet backing.

"Yes, do watch out for him; he is ruthless."

"How did these guys grab power?" I asked. "I was working somewhere else back in '79," I hastily added. Christ, I was getting an intelligence briefing from a guy who was possibly a Canadian intelligence officer, and it was still my first hour in Central America. This was beyond my wildest dreams, and I certainly didn't want to blow it. If he wanted to think I was an American intelligence agent, then let him.

"Well, the uprising against Somoza was actually long overdue," he said. "Somoza was U.S.-trained, in fact, a West Pointer kept in power by America. He ran the country as if it were his family's feudal estate, which it might as well have been.

"He had his Guardia Nacional to keep people in line and things went along smoothly for years, at least as far as the Somozas and the rest of the oligarchy were concerned. He had the good sense not to molest the Indians, though. They were allowed to conduct their own tribal government, courts, and churches.

"Of course for anyone with democratic tendencies of any stripe, life could get rough in Somoza's Nicaragua. He kept order and suppressed dissent. Still, even with Carter in the White House, he could have kept his power, but a few of his Guardia Nacional killed a sacred cow—an American *periodista*. After that journalist was killed and it was actually shown on U.S. television, even American conservatives couldn't defend Somoza any longer. Your President cut off aid.

"The rebels who had been fighting in the hills and jungles for years were joined by disillusioned moderates and liberals. The end came quickly, and Somoza fled to Miami.

"You know, of course, that they terminated him?"

"Oh, yes," I assured him.

He went on, "The Communists classically subverted the pluralistic revolution. The democratic groups in the anti-Somoza front, led by patriots like Robelo and Calero, were relegated to minor roles or barred from the new government by the Frente Sandino Liberacion Nacional.

"Poor Robelo. He came home one day to find his house redecorated with garbage, his car vandalized, and his family jeered at and threatened by Sandinista hoodlums. Robelo is not a stupid man. He left Nicaragua.

"The FSLN continued their campaign of terror and tightened their grip on the country. Democratic dissidents without the stature of a Robelo simply disappeared, thousands of them. Before long the Sandinistas had consolidated their power. The nine commandantes of the FSLN *are* the government of Nicaragua."

"Who is this guy Sandino?" I asked.

The Canadian looked at me with a frown, as if to say "Why haven't you done your homework?" But he shrugged and went on, "Augusto Cesar Sandino was a peasant leader who led an armed struggle against your Marine Corps when they occupied Nicaragua back in the twenties and thirties, after United Fruit and some of the other companies had problems down here.

"When the Marines were finally being withdrawn, Sandino was lured out of the hills and attended a banquet to celebrate the arrival of self-government. After the dinner the Somoza family, who had been installed by the Marines as leaders of the new government, had a surprise for Sandino. He was assassinated.

"Sandino was a populist of sorts, some would even call him a Communist. But he was as Nicaraguan as rice and beans, and even some of the non-Marxist groups claim ideological descent from Sandino. Don't take that name in vain when you're in Nicaragua, m'boy. He ranks as high with some Nicaraguans as George Washington does with your people."

A flight to Panama was announced and the Canadian rose to depart.

"Luck to you, m'boy. And keep your head

down." He winked, turned, and strode down the concourse with athletic grace and speed.

Well, I thought, *here you are in Central America, a paddle fan turning slowly above you, a strong rum drink in your hand, head spinning with facts given you gratis by a man who is quite likely an intelligence agent from a friendly power, and you haven't even reached your destination yet. You're certainly off to a good start, John.*

CHAPTER FOUR

NICARAGUA

When the plane touched down I could see the gray, cracked, rutted runway illuminated by landing lights. The damage looked bad enough to be sabotage, but I remembered the Canadian had said this was a Communist country. Possibly nobody worked full-time except the police.

The strip at Augusto C. Sandino International Airport was lined with American H-34 choppers and T-33 jet trainers, visible in cones of green-tinted security lights. I tried to count aircraft as I walked down the stained, wheeled stair with the typical Latin mix of airline passengers: returning vacationers—affluent and politically connected, no doubt—businessmen, foreign tourists, and an American family reporting to a new assignment at the embassy.

As we formed the slow queue for customs inspection, we were told all foreigners entering the country must purchase sixty dollars' worth of Nicaraguan currency at the official exchange rate: ten *cordobas* to the dollar. The bank rate at the time was twenty to one and the black market offered one hundred to one. We were just supporting their government's balance-of-payments deficit. However, it is never wise to argue with foreign officials. I handed over my money.

Passport control and customs in Nicaragua are manned by the Ejercito Popular Sandino, the Sandinista People's Army. I was surprised at the cursory inspection. They just looked at my open luggage, closed it, and waved me through.

Clearing customs, I went outside and was set upon by a small mob of children clamoring for my attention and my *cordobas*.

"Dame algo, dame algo," they screeched.

I motioned for the three skinniest children to take my bags and followed them to a taxi. When I gave them each an American dollar thirty more hands stretched out toward me.

"Norteamericano, dame algo," they demanded.

The taxi ride to the Inter-Continental cost most of my new *cordobas*, and I found the hotel room expensive by Central American standards, about fifty-five dollars a night. Single room: no television and a radio that didn't work, but an excellent view of the army post next door.

I found my way to the bar after unpacking and was invited to join a table of Nicaraguans who told me they were attorneys. They insisted that Spanish be spoken, but all three asked me for an American cigarette. When I replied that I did not smoke they suggested I buy them each a pack.

Not wishing to offend citizens of a host country, but also not wishing to be hustled, I politely declined, stating that I did not traffic in tobacco for ethical reasons. I spared them my usual lecture on the hazards of smoking.

They assailed me with questions about President Reagan's hostility toward the Sandinista regime and tried to outdo each other in assuring me that the present government was the best that Nicaragua had ever enjoyed, that times were truly good and going to get better if the gringos would just leave them alone. They did allow, however, that the better times might be two or three generations in arriving. In the next breaths they asked me to buy them drinks and sheepishly admitted that they had no money.

The waiter who had come over to the table to take my order sneered at them, *"Abogados sin dinero."*

A few patrons at other tables occasionally glanced our way. With each such look one of my companions would loudly proclaim, *"Yo creo en la revolucion,"* thereby affirming himself as a good Sandinista who believed in the revolution . . . the revolution that apparently had taken the money from his pockets.

I shook off the entreaties of my would-be drinking buddies and went to the Inter-Continental's dining room. A *plato tipico* strongly resembled the good, country cooking on which I was raised.

After dinner I sat in a rattan armchair in the red-cloth and dark-wood hotel lounge, sipping a drink strong with cheap Cuban rum and observing the other guests. There were quite a few

Americans, including Tom Wicker of *The New York Times* and some staffers for two Democratic congressmen. Snatches of conversation drifted my way:

"Commandante Ortega's commitment to the poor . . ."

"Human rights improvement . . ."

"Resumption of aid . . ."

I noticed a poster in the hotel's corridors that advertised a demonstration the next day in front of the American Embassy. The poster went on to express fervent hope that all Americans in Managua would attend and protest the Reagan Administration's support of anti-Sandinista rebels, known to the world as Contras, short for counterrevolutionary in Spanish.

I wouldn't miss it for the world.

The next day I decided to tour Managua. Leaving the hotel, I refused the entreaties of the taxi drivers and walked through the city with my camera, making my way to the embassy. Just as the long-haired, sandaled demonstrators arrived, the skies opened up and the sudden tropical downpour soaked us all. The sight of these bedraggled protestors with their limp, soggy posters provided comic relief from the rest of somber Nicaragua.

I returned to the Hotel Inter-Continental, dried off, and changed clothes. After lunch I returned to my walking tour of Managua. I noticed the absence of vehicles in the capital city's streets. Nothing but taxis, Sandinista officials in

chauffeured Mercedes limousines, and some large
army trucks of East German manufacture.

I found the Inturismo office in a park near the
hotel and inquired about the sights Managua
might offer a gringo tourist. The first thing I discovered there was that the Inturismo guides
spoke no English. Nor did they speak Italian or
French. While I stood there practicing my Spanish with the beautiful Nicaraguan guide, tourists
of those nationalities walked away muttering to
themselves, unable to get any information.

"The Inturismo jobs go to loyal Sandinistas,"
the guide told me. She then sold me a map of the
city for the remainder of my *cordobas*.

I explored the city on my own, taking pictures
of some of the anti-American graffiti, hammer-
and-sickle billboards, the ruins of the once-im-
pressive national cathedral, troops marching
through the streets, lines in front of the shops,
and various other sights that only a Communist
country has to offer. The earthquake-damaged
sidewalk resembled a roller coaster, and walking
was made even more taxing by the oppressive humidity. Compared to Central America, Florida is
dry and cool.

On the way back to the hotel I stopped to photograph a bungalow—a classic example of Latin
American architecture—that had a sign in the
front yard proclaiming that this was the Ricardo
Morales Aviles House. In the center of the sign
was a hat like Tom Mix used to wear in the old
cowboy movies that I saw for nine cents in my
childhood and the letters *FSLN*. The hat was a

symbol of Sandino and the letters stood for Frente Sandino Liberacion Nacional.

Unknowingly, I had just taken a picture of one of the headquarters of the Sandinista party.

I started to walk on after clicking a few more shots, but a pimply-faced youth of eighteen strode out of the *casa* and beckoned for me to come into the house. I feigned ignorance and tried to move on down the shattered sidewalk. But he beckoned again and pointed to the .45-caliber automatic stuck in his belt.

I followed him into the house, where my passport and camera were taken from me. I was then questioned by a short, bearded man who had the look of a professor. He asked me who I was, what I was doing in Nicaragua, why I was taking a picture of the house, and other questions that I tried to answer politely in my very best Spanish. He went into an office and returned with a stocky, swarthy man whom he introduced as the commandante of the house. My new interrogator asked me if I knew what sort of house I was in. I admitted that I did not. He proceeded to tell me that the house was a former holding of the dictator Anastasio Somoza, that it had been liberated by the people, and was now headquarters of the youth branch of the Sandinista Liberation Front.

He went on to tell me that the house had been the target of a recent attack by Contras.

"I am sorry for the inconvenience, Senor," he apologized. "But we will have to detain you while we verify your passport and identity." He and the professor left me.

While I was waiting in the outer office two Americans came in, spoke to the receptionist in rapid-fire Spanish, and were politely ushered into the commandante's office. The only words I could make out were "Washington, D.C." and "mutual concerns."

After an hour and a half of detention I grew tired of watching two young punks posture about the room with pistols in their belts. I was getting irritated and antsy. My mind flashed to the training of Grand Master Song and I entertained myself with a daydream in which I slap-kicked the pistols from their waistbands, spun around, and smashed double back-fists into their pimpled faces, then leapt across the room to put a flying side snap-kick into the receptionist's throat before she could reach the telephone. After this free *Tae Kwon Do* lesson for the Sandinista punks, I would . . .

Fortunately, Grand Master Song did not train fools. I contented myself with fantasy action, especially after I spotted the television camera secreted in a corner. I was under constant observation from outside as well as within the room. My thoughts took on a more contemplative turn as I cooled my heels and waited.

The commandante and the professor returned with my passport and camera. They told me I was free to go, but cautioned me against taking any more pictures while in Managua. The camera, of course, was empty. Fortunately I had popped out the film cartridge and replaced it with an unexposed roll while following the young Sandinista into the house.

I didn't consider myself a coward and I'd heard more than a few shots fired in anger, some of them aimed at me, but I had to admit that I felt real fear after leaving the Ricardo Morales Aviles House, similar to the trembling that often follows a near miss on an interstate.

I remembered the whispers around the hotel about another American who had been arrested a few days previously. He had been carrying three passports—all in different names. To the best of my knowledge, he was never heard from again. I knew that I, too, could have disappeared into the Sandinista Gulag.

CHAPTER FIVE

HOW DO I GET OUT OF HERE?

The pyramidal shape of the Hotel Inter-Continental looked almost friendly. As soon as I closed the room door and locked it, I called to give Alexandra an update and let her know that my position may have become precarious.

While I was still pumping myself up for this career change, we had gone to see the movie *Dogs of War*. The hero of this film about mercenaries was detained while making a reconnaissance of the target country. His savage captors beat him. But later he returned at the head of an assault force and exacted revenge while fulfilling an assignment.

Before my detention by the Sandinistas, phone calls to the United States went through in about forty-five seconds. However, this call took forty-five minutes before I heard the familiar voice.

"Do you remember the movie about Africa?" I queried.

Alexandra replied in the affirmative.

"Well, remember what happened when Christopher Walken visited that country?"

She was silent for a long moment. "Yes, I remember."

"It just happened to me . . . only I didn't get the full treatment," I added, to assure her that I hadn't been beaten or tortured.

"I'm going to try to get a flight out of here tomorrow to San Jose, Costa Rica, but I might not be able to get a seat. So I'll check in with you each day until I'm out of here. If you don't hear from me by midnight of any day, call the duty officer at the State Department Bureau of Intelligence." I gave her the phone number and hoped it would keep the listening Sandinista security agents off my ass.

"Now that I've ruined your night's sleep, I'm going to try to get some myself. I'll talk to you tomorrow."

"Please be careful, John."

I assured her that I'd try to keep out of further trouble, chuckled at the echoes on the telephone, and hung up. I told myself that I deserved a drink after the day's ordeal and went downstairs to the hotel bar after exchanging more dollars for the local currency at the front desk.

Cuban rum is plentiful and cheap in Nicaragua. Putting politics aside, I ordered a double on the rocks.

Soon after settling in at the bar, I was joined by a short, squat but well-dressed Latino who turned to me and said, "Hi, buddy, you can talk English to me."

I thought that this was obviously a Sandinista functionary who had been assigned to keep an eye on me. He proceeded to tell me a few things about myself, details of my past life, my address in Florida, and the license-plate number of my Corvette.

"Do you want me to tell you the number on the Florida driver's license in your wallet?" he smirked.

I was impressed.

"You know," he went on, still smirking, "you should be ashamed of yourself about Vietnam."

I lowered my head and muttered, "I am sorry about Vietnam."

A grin split his face. "Really? You're sorry about Vietnam?"

"Yes, I'm sorry we didn't turn the fucking place into a parking lot."

The grin left his face and was replaced by a steely mask of hate. He hissed through clenched teeth, "You Americans. You always think of force."

Since the gloves seemed to be off, I asked him about the large military establishment maintained by his country.

"That's your fault," he said. "We are threatened by the United States and your President's support of the Contras. We must defend our revolution."

"What kind of revolution is it that produces such poverty?" I asked.

He replied, "We are a poor country because of American imperialism. Your companies extracted goods and resources and paid us shit! They exploited the workers and peasants, working them like slaves for a few cents a day."

"That's ancient history," I scoffed. "How about a little freedom, since we're on the subject of revolution. That's what ours was all about."

"Everyone is free in Nicaragua," he countered. "Except for the Somocistas."

"Bullshit! I was arrested today for taking pictures."

"You weren't arrested," he snapped. "You were detained."

I realized that I was on thin ice, but wasn't about to back off. "Call it what you want," I snapped back.

"Why do you want to kill us?" he asked me.

"I don't want to kill anyone. I'm in Central America to assess the situation for myself. Then I hope to find some type of work helping the people of this region obtain the economic and political freedom they deserve."

"You can help Nicaragua achieve economic freedom," he said. "Why don't you volunteer to work in one of our coffee warehouses?"

I pictured myself humping hundred kilo sacks of coffee for the Sandinistas. "I'll think about that," I told him.

Sure I would.

Thinking it was time to escape, I told the Sandinista that the strong Cuban rum was getting to my head and that I was going to bed. He sat, sullen and silent, without acknowledging my wave as I feigned a stagger, with little effort, and left the bar.

I slept late the next day, finally awakened by the maid pounding on my door.

"Senor, son las dos en la tarde. I must clean the room," she yelled.

"Aaaargh," I groaned. "No wonder those Cubans are such mean bastards."

While the maid restored order to my room I fumbled for aspirin in a bag. I rooted through bottles of sulfa drugs, antibiotics, and vitamins before I found what my aching head was demanding.

"Senor, dame algo."

What the hell, I thought. *That must be the national slogan—'Give me something.'*

"No hay leche, Senor. For the children, give to me one time the vitamins. *Por favor, Senor."*

I gave her a bottle of multivitamins.

My feet hurt from the walking tour of the day before. And last night's rum was still shorting out half the synapses in my central nervous system. My heart's slow, irregular beats put unwelcome pressure on the backs of my eyeballs. I decided on a taxi tour. The first stop was the Aeronica office, where I was told that no seats were available on that day's flight to San José.

"Your reservations are for Tuesday. Why do you wish to leave Managua so soon?" The clerk smirked.

I choked back the angry response that rose to my lips and mumbled something about important business in Costa Rica.

"Check with us each day, Senor, perhaps we can find a seat for you before Tuesday."

Back in the Ford that had obviously served its owner for more years than anyone had a right to expect, I asked for a tour of the city. My driver was almost a caricature of the image most gringos have of Latins: fat and ebullient, with dark skin that glistened with oily sweat. But his boyish enthusiasm for life dispelled any stereotype in my mind.

"Do many *norteamericanos* come to Managua?" I asked him.

"No, Senor, not now. Not like in the Somoza days," he replied.

"*Hay Rusos?*" I inquired. *What the hell*, I thought. *I might as well go for it.*

I half expected him to head for the nearest police station and denounce me as a CIA spy, but instead he answered, "*No hay muchos. Pero, Bulgaros . . . hijo puta,* those Bulgarians are cheap bastards."

Feeling that I was on a roll, I pressed on. "*Y Cubanos? Hay muchos Cubanos en Nicaragua?*"

"*Bastante!*" he barked.

When a Nicaraguan says "Enough!" he means it as an understatement.

The amiable driver went on to tell me about his vacation trip to Cuba. Travel to Castro's island was cheap and encouraged by the Sandinistas. At that time a seven-day trip from Managua to Havana, including round-trip airfare, hotel, some of your meals, and sight-seeing tours, could be had for a little over one hundred American dollars. The man had been shocked at the corruption, but disillusionment had been overshadowed by the girls he enjoyed.

"Putas negras con culos grandes!" he chortled. "Black whores with big asses!" His dark eyes flashed as he grinned at the memory. Spittle flecked the windshield as he panted. Then, perhaps thinking that he had been remiss in not asking me sooner, he turned and inquired solicitiously, "Do you require a woman, Senor?" It was the most elegant solicitation I'd ever heard.

"Si, como no?" I told him. Hell, Alexandra probably wasn't going to come down anyway. "Why not?" I chuckled at my rationalization and wondered what a Nicaraguan bordello was going to be like.

Club Tropicana was hardly jumping when I arrived. It's a huge dance hall and bar on the southeastern outskirts of Managua. Only five of the two hundred-odd tables were occupied. Two girls joined me at the table, hustling drinks and massaging my thighs. After a half hour or so of drinking, dancing, and being fondled, I went to relieve my bladder.

Worn cushions on creaking booths and unwaxed floors in the roller-rink-sized dance hall showed how things weren't working, but few things tell you maintenance isn't being done like a Central American urinal. You walk in, unzip, and experimentally establish an angle of incidence between stream and wall that doesn't splash your shoes. Even a gutter would help, but the usual Central American pissoir just has the angle between wall and floor to carry waste away.

As similar systems from Birmingham to Bangkok show, it can work. But when temperatures and humidity are high, tile isn't cleaned regularly, and nobody takes the trouble to clean and patch, urine soaks into the grout and works like spray-mist deodorizer that spits ammonia instead of perfume.

It was sobering. I needed another drink.

I returned to find the two whores gone and a statuesque Latina sitting at my table. She was tall and slender; her face looked as if it had been lifted off a Mayan temple.

Classic! I thought.

I gestured quizzically toward the empty chairs.

"You didn't want them," she told me. Her voice was clear and musical and her Spanish lacked the guttural harshness of many Nicaragüense.

"Yes, I did."

"No, they would just try to steal your money. Sit, I will be your companion tonight. *Me llama Maria.*"

I obeyed the gentle command and thought that the expression "getting lucky" had just taken on dramatic new meaning.

"You speak English?" I was tired, very close to being drunk . . . and a little suspicious.

"Que dices tu?"

"Habla espanol solamente?"

No, she didn't speak English; no, she didn't work at the bordello; and, no again, she wasn't a

Sandinista. Besides, she was too pretty to be political, I thought. With a fifth of rum in my system, I just didn't want to believe a beautiful girl was hustling me for any reason.

I led her to the dance floor and realized that the rum was certainly affecting my performance there. I thought we better leave soon or another type of performance would soon be endangered.

Maria said she was ready. She helped me out of the bar and into a waiting taxi.

"Inter-Continental," I slurred to the driver. *"Cual es la tarifa?"*

"Mil cordobas, Senor," he replied. "One thousand *cordobas."*

"Ladron!" Maria snapped. She unleashed a torrent of abuse at the driver. I couldn't have followed it if I'd been sober. Her invective then took on a cold, menacing tone and the taxi driver blanched.

"Si, si, companera," he stammered.

At the hotel I fumbled for a thousand-*cordoba* note and the unfortunate driver paled even more. *"No, Senor. Gratis, gratis."* His tires squealed as the cab roared out of the circular drive.

I remember thinking it strange that a cab driver in Central America should give a gringo a free ride, especially when the price he quoted had been the expected rip-off rate. But the sight of Maria's rounded bottom under her tight gown as she walked up the hotel's steps interrupted my analysis and I followed her into the lobby.

Before the door to my room had closed behind us, our hands were at each other's clothes. The

heat and passion of Central America flowed between us as our bodies merged in carnal lust. The
new world I'd entered—the world of intrigue and
secret agents, where people can be snatched off
the street and disappear, where the East–West
struggle is played out with bullets instead of
words—had created tension in me that sought release in the body of the Mayan princess that
writhed beneath me. "Sandinista bitch . . . I'll
show you . . . American imperialism. . . . It's
us . . . fucking the world. . . . And making
them . . . love it. . . . Just like you're . . .
loving this. . . . You hot little . . . *Sandinista*
bitch." Her hips rose to meet mine with each
thrust until we exploded together in almost painful climax.

I collapsed, panting. She put her arms around
me and I fell asleep immediately.

The next morning as she dressed I searched my
pockets for *cordobas* to give her. When I had assembled what seemed an appropriate amount, I
held them out to her with an embarrassed
"Gracias."

"No, keep your money, John. But thank you
for an enjoyable evening," she said in unaccented
English.

Two days later I was able to wangle a standby
seat on an Aeronica flight to San José, Costa
Rica. This time my luggage received more than
the token examination it had received when I entered the country. Six khaki-clad EPS troopers
descended upon my bags and rifled them vigorously. When one of them came across my jungle-

style combat boots, he held them aloft and cried triumphantly, *"Militar!"*

I heard muttered fragments of conversation between the soldiers:

"Hijo puta gringo . . ."

"Mercenario . . ."

"Enemigo del pueblo . . ."

Then they sullenly stuffed my gear back in the bags and, surprisingly, waved me through. It may be that the Sandinistas were as anxious to get rid of me as I was to get out of there.

On July 24, 1983, I left Managua.

CHAPTER SIX

THE CONTRAS

Smiling officials from the Department of Tourism greeted arriving passengers at the Juan Santamaria International Airport. I was welcomed to Costa Rica, asked if I had anything to declare, and passed through customs without even having to open a bag.

I settled into the back of a four-door Datsun taxi.

The chrome on the door handle flaked, but it was slick and clean. The same slickness—probably spray cleaner—made the light blue vinyl look silver in the light. Dark blue nylon shag had been cut to cover the original plastic floormats, and it all reeked of spray cleaning fluid and tobacco smoke. Harsh sunlight was dimmed by the reflective film covering half the windshield with the word *RALLYE* spelled out on the top strip. Green-and-white woven tape with tasseled balls had been glued around the edge of the windshield. A small gilt bronze Christopher hung from the rearview mirror, a three-inch-long imitation-enamel Virgin medal was glued to the center of the dash, and a Renaissance painting of Joseph at his bench, cut from a magazine, was cellophane-taped to the glove-box door. It was, in other words, a typical south-of-the-border taxicab.

As we headed into the city I chatted with the amiable *"Tico"* cabbie about the healthy state of the Costa Rican economy. We drove past factories, trucks loaded with goods, shopping centers with full parking lots, and other signs of thriving commerce along the divided highway leading from the airport to the city of San José.

When I mentioned that I had just come from Managua, his face clouded and he murmured, *"Muy triste, muy triste."*

He told me that Costa Rica was being flooded with refugees from their neighbor to the north. Many Costa Ricans are related by blood to Nicaraguan families and the ties between the people of the two countries are strong even when their governments are clashing.

Of course this holds true throughout Central America; nothing happens in or to one country without an effect on its neighbors.

The taxi driver explained this to me in simple, precise terms that belied his formal education. He'd spent eight years in school, which he proudly told me was required and free in Costa Rica.

The cabbie wasn't telling me anything I didn't know, but hearing it from a man-on-the-street was interesting. Third World peasants are often more politically sophisticated than American university graduates.

The ride was a good teacher . . . even better than the cabbie. If anyone is interested in a short course in comparative government, the flight from Managua to San José and a day in each city should earn college credits.

San José bustled; people shopped; they bought and sold; they laughed and smiled.

In Managua the predominant mood had been sadness. People moped about the *mercados*, which, though filled with produce and goods, had few buyers.

My first stop on San José, after checking in at the posh Hotel Cariari, was an American bar known as the Key Largo. It sits on the corner across from the Parque Morazon in downtown San José. The Key Largo has been described by one foreign correspondent as "one of the world's greatest bars" and by another as "a gloomy mansion where one is set upon by aggressive tarts." Either way, it sounded like an interesting spot. The twin ideas of drinking in one of the world's great bars and being set upon by an aggressive tart were both acceptable. And I'd heard the place was a hangout for everyone from visiting businessmen to CIA case officers and mercenary soldiers.

I was not disappointed. The darkness of the place was accented by the mahogany of the bar and paneling; paddle fans stirred the thick air, and Central Casting couldn't have filled the

wicker chairs around the tables with more inter-
esting-looking characters.

The first person I met there was a retired Los
Angeles *Times* reporter, Jerry Ruhlow. We sipped
icy bottles of Imperial, the favorite local brew,
and conversed. I told him I was a psychologist
from Florida, studying the refugee problems
throughout the Caribbean Basin countries. I produced a letter on state university stationery
signed by a nonexistent dean attesting to this.

He suggested that I talk to Orion Pastora, a
cousin of Commander Zero, about what their exile group was doing to help the refugees. I obtained the address of their office from another
periodista who worked for the *Tico Times*, a leftist, English-language paper that catered to the
expatriate community in Costa Rica.

The offices were located in the western suburbs
of the city. They housed the political and press
liaison sections of the resistance group. Military
headquarters were several kilometers farther out
of the city, on a heavily guarded *estancia.*

Sandinistas had just tried to bomb the Contra
group's office. Two terrorists were carrying an ex-
plosive device to be planted near their enemy's
headquarters when the radio signal from a pass-
ing taxi triggered it and blew them to hell. Security was tight after that.

I arrived there at a bad time, the security
guards told me. Orion Pastora was not in, nor was
any other politician who could talk to me. However, a visiting free-lance journalist from Italy
volunteered his services. This serendipitous meet-

ing with Marcantonio, like the chance encounter with the Canadian "insurance broker," helped me make my way through the Byzantine world of Central American politics.

Marcantonio spoke excellent English, Spanish, German, and French . . . as well as Italian. I later learned, when he took me to a luncheon at the Italian Embassy in San José, that he was a contract agent for the Italian Secret Service. He had completed a deep-penetration assignment of several years duration in Nicaragua early in 1983. He had even taken a Nicaraguan wife to protect his cover. When his mission had been blown by Cuban agents of the Direccion General de Intelligenica, he had escaped Nicaragua hidden in the baggage of a Brazilian diplomat. He had been a paratrooper in the Italian Army, although his appearance—five foot three, a hundred and ten pounds soaking wet—belied his profession and history. Marcantonio was engaging, mild-mannered, and harmless-looking. Probably perfect cover for his danger-filled life.

After I'd gotten to know him I had asked the diminutive Italian why his country was so concerned about political events in this hemisphere.

He responded readily, "John, you know that Italy is a relatively poor country. Yet, because we are good Catholics, there are many Italians—many more than the land or our industries can support. The answer for many Italians seeking to better themselves is emigration. Your own country has millions of citizens that are of Italian descent. But our emigrants go to other countries too—Nicaragua, Argentina, Costa Rica, Chile, just to name a few.

"Italy does not forget her sons and daughters just because they live in a foreign land. We maintain an interest in their welfare and, therefore, we are concerned with political and economic conditions in the countries to which they have emigrated. This interest isn't altruistic, John, don't think that. The practicality is that these people send money home to their poorer relatives, and it all adds up to a sizable portion of our foreign exchange.

"Did you happen to notice that, even though they are partners in NATO and the European Economic Community, Italy did not support Great Britain in what you English-speaking people call the Falklands War?"

"I do remember something about that. Not much I'm afraid," I admitted.

"Did you know that over half of the Argentine sailors who died when the British submarine torpedoed the *General Belgrano* were of Italian descent? I'm not arguing the rights or wrongs of that war, John, it's outside my area of operations, but I do have my opinions. But I digress. Have I answered your question, my friend?"

He had.

The Italian asked for my credentials when I told him why I had come to the Contra offices. He studied everything in my wallet from my passport and a DD 214—certifying my most recent honorable separation from active duty in the U.S.

Army—to my membership card from the Florida Association of Practicing Psychologists.

He then assured the security officers that I was indeed a visiting professional and an American veteran who was interested in rendering some sort of assistance to their cause. I added that I had been in Managua and had been arrested by the FSLN a few days before. This revelation gave me instant credibility. As I, and any world traveler can attest, international paperwork is meaningless, and these hombres knew it. Credentials can be purchased or forged, but a Sandinista arrest record is something you have to work for.

The chief of security gave me the address of another office, more remote, where I could find Orion Pastora. He called ahead to inform them that I had been cleared and was on the way. Marcantonio again volunteered his services as guide and translator and accompanied me to Orion's office. Orion Pastora was the press liaison and public information officer of the democratic alliance. I was later told that he owed his position solely to his relationship to Commander Zero and that he was almost universally disliked, not only by the press corps, but by the other Contras.

Marcantonio introduced me to the corpulent Orion, and since we were dealing with sensitive issues requiring a Spanish vocabulary that I did not have, he suggested that I speak my piece in English and let him translate to Pastora. I gratefully agreed and told Pastora of my experiences with the Sandinistas and my desire to join in their struggle against this despotic enemy.

Orion told me I could visit Commander Zero at a camp inside Nicaragua but that I could not stay and I could not fight. I explained to him that my interests did not lie in visiting or reporting this war, that I was not a journalist but a soldier, and wished to become a part of the war. I reiterated that I shared their enmity with the Sandinistas, that I believed in the cause of democracy, and was willing to fight for this belief.

Orion was not impressed and repeated his offer of a brief visit to a base camp.

We left Orion's office and returned to downtown San José. As the tiny Italian left for his pension, he turned and invited me to join him watching a soccer game that evening between the Costa Rican national team and a visiting squad from Poland.

I accepted and met him later that evening at the stadium in La Sabana park near the San José suburb of Pavas. Marcantonio's press credentials got us excellent seats.

Skillful dribbling and flashy passes abounded, and everybody hugged everybody else every couple of minutes. But nothing showed on the scoreboard, so there was time to talk. I questioned my new friend about the organization and motivation of the Contras' Democratic Alliance. Marcantonio was a gold mine of information. He gave me a scorecard for the resistance groups and explained the confusing political differences among the refugee groups in Central America. I pumped him for all he was worth. He seemed ea-

ger to share his information with an American
and needed little encouragement.

The Alliance, he told me, had been formed by
Nicaraguan refugees from the Sandinista regime
who had fled to neighboring Costa Rica. The original Alliance consisted of Misurasata, a Sandino-
oriented organization of the indigenous tribes of
Miskito, Sumo, and Rama Indians led by a young
Indian named Brooklyn Rivera. Pastora's group,
the Frente Revolucionario Sandino, the Movimiento Democratico Nicaraguense, led by Alfonso Robelo, and the Union Democratico Nicaraguense of Fernando "El Negro" Chamorro
made up the original Alliance.

"You see, John, unlike the Nicaraguan government, the resistance represents a broad section of
the political spectrum." That hadn't occurred to
me.

"Then what are they all fighting the central
government for?"

"Because the revolution promised . . . what
do you call it? Oh, yes, 'pluralistic democracy.'
You know—the idea that competitive groups can
participate in the same government."

"I knew they had frozen out the right, but are
you telling me they cut out leftists too?"

"Why, yes! That is why the Sandinistas are in
such trouble with the counterrevolutionary forces
—there are too many 'enemies of the revolution.'
You see, as long as you are a Cuban-style Communist Latino, you are franchised in today's Nicaragua. If you are an Indian or a liberal or any
other type of leftist, you are not represented. If

the Sandinistas fought only the Nicaraguan conservatives, there would be no trouble at all."

"Do the rebel groups break down on these political and ethnic lines?"

"Very much so. This group's politics are those of the liberal Democrats in the United States. However, even within the Contra alliance there is a range of political orientation much broader than that of the Sandinistas. Pastora's FRS represents the extreme left, and UDN the more conservative element, like U.S.-style moderate Republicans."

"So the Sandinistas have made the government their exclusive property when the revolution wasn't," I pondered aloud. "That's what the Contras mean when they say the FSLN has betrayed the revolution." That certainly jibed with what the Canadian had told me in El Salvador.

"You have it exactly. My friend, half the combatants from the last revolution must be back out in the field. There aren't more because many are embittered by the failure of the last revolution. It's just like revolutionary Russia—a well-organized minority has stolen the revolution of the people. And it must be remembered that Pastora has some of the same inclinations as his former friends in the FSLN, and good men are leaving the alliance because of him."

"You mean, soldiers leaving the field, or what?"

"Well, that, of course, but there are organizational defections too. One of the great men of the battle for Nicaragua is Negro Chamorro. The

word is that his men are so dissatisfied with Eden
Pastora and with Pastora blocking Chamorro
from his rightful leadership of his faction, that El
Negro will be forced to withdraw from the alliance."

"Chamorro is black?" I was surprised.

"No." Marcantonio laughed. "No! It's like
nicknaming someone 'Blackie' in English. Chamorro is just swarthier than the average Nicaraguan."

While our neighbors screamed and a lone Costa
Rican player threw himself across the path of
what had seemed a certain goal, Marcantonio
pulled a sheaf of papers from his inside jacket
pocket. When the noise died down and normal
play resumed, he handed me the papers. "This is
the Democratic Alliance's political platform.
Read it carefully. Insofar as any distillation can
be—this is true. If you join, you will kill and may
die for what is represented here. Be sure you can
live with what is written in this document."

The game raged on and the fans howled with
unabashed Nationalistic fury while I read. The
platform was made of eighteen planks:

  1) an authentic pluralistic government;
  2) national sovereignty and nonalignment;
  3) a mixture of private, state, and community
     efforts in the economy;
  4) social programs;
  5) freedom of expression;
  6) freedom of assembly and organization;
  7) free public education;

8) the establishment of a junta to govern for a maximum of one year;

9) separation of powers within the state;

10) a guarantee of free election no less than one year after the installation of the revolutionary junta;

11) the establishment of a national constituent assembly;

12) the establishment of a nonideological armed force;

13) a process for the establishment of laws and amendments;

14) the repeal of laws permitting confiscation of property;

15) reconciliation of the various political parties;

16) a just policy toward the Indians;

17) agrarian reform by the creation of independent cooperative farms; and last,

18) the establishment of a nonpartisan civil service system.

"Well," I told Marcantonio after reading the document. "There's certainly nothing in here that offends my political sensibilities. In fact, I think it offensive that a government exists in that country that doesn't guarantee these rights or propose these laws."

"Ah! A fine pass," he remarked. "Their political instability frightens me, but the Poles can certainly play soccer. But forgive me, John, as a Latin I am as excited by *futbol* as any *campesino* here. Please continue."

"What about this group, FDN? American papers say that they're backed by the CIA."

"For once your papers are telling you the truth," he responded. "The *Fuerzas Democraticas Nicaraguense* are a creation of your Central Intelligence Agency. They represent the conservative elements of the Nicaraguan body politic: churchmen, businessmen, even former Guardia Nacional officers. At this time they have about ten thousand fighting men, well equipped and well trained. They are based in Honduras and fight strictly on the northern border of Nicaragua. With their trained leaders, CIA-provided weapons and training, they're more of a threat to the Sandinistas than the forces of the Democratic Alliance."

We then settled back to enjoy the rest of the game. The locals had two superstars who kept the crowd leaping to its feet and cheering their heroics, but the efficient Poles eventually wore down the enthusiastic Costa Ricans and blanked them with a 3–0 final score.

Later, Marcantonio introduced me to many of the Contra leaders and to members of the rank and file. One of the most impressive Nicaraguan patriots I met during my days at headquarters was Cesar Aviles, a workhorse who had learned to meet the logistical needs of a military force and train recruits in the use of the Chinese-made RPG-7 rocket launcher. His background, however, included degrees in law and engineering rather than military science.

In early August 1983 I met with Alfonso Robelo in the alliance's San José offices. Robelo is an engineer and a politician. I mean, he kisses

babies, he smiles, shakes hands, and says he's glad
to see you. He's a real politician in the American
sense and he even looks the part. Tall, handsome,
and cultivated, he has the kind of face you almost
expect to see on a billboard or a poster.

From all the reports that I was privy to, he is
also a man of honor, integrity, and an unshakable
belief in democracy. You could add "courage" to
his list of attributes. Robelo had been the target
of several assassination attempts since he escaped
to Costa Rica, including one by a team of international assassins from a Basque terrorist group,
and he's never even slowed down in his efforts to
free his country. Interestingly, the Basques had
journeyed from Moscow to Managua prior to entering Costa Rica.

At my Italian friend's suggestion, and with his
help, I had prepared a proposal, written in Spanish, offering my service to the democratic forces.
The proposal documented my interest in Latin
American affairs, my experiences with communism's effects on the Cubans and Vietnamese, my
desire to fight for a free Nicaragua, and a request
that they guarantee me a contract to provide security services after the war.

This was presented to Robelo, who received it
graciously. He would personally contact Commander Zero by radio to tell him of my offer and
of his own approval.

Several days went by with no word from Zero.
When I asked about the status of my offer I was
told that I would have to be cleared by the military security detachment.

Well, this made sense. And I certainly had nothing to hide from people whom I had asked to trust me in armed conflict. An appointment was made with the security detachment.

At the time the head of security was Adolfo "Popo" Chamorro, a fearsome figure of a man. His eyes mirrored the struggles his body and soul had endured in the years of warfare, first against Somoza, then against the betrayers of that revolution. Popo was over six feet, whip-thin, and hard. His shaven head and cold, unblinking eyes made all but the most secure and well-adjusted feel ill at ease. "Dr. Death" was my private nickname for this steely-eyed counterrevolutionary.

I was also interviewed by "El Gringo," another security officer whose primary interest was in my military background and what I had to offer in terms of training and combat experience. They both seemed happy with my background and motivation and recommended to San Pedro, the military headquarters, that I be accepted as a member of the armed forces of the Democratic Alliance.

Days passed and I was eventually told the final decision would be up to Pastora and that he would be contacted by radio with the entire proposal.

While waiting for Pastora's decision I was invited to take part in some of the group's refugee relief work. I accepted an invitation to carry supplies to a refugee camp near Limón on the Atlantic coast of Costa Rica.

On the Sunday following my security inter-

view, Marcantonio, some Creole members of the
exile group, and I loaded up a rented Russian-
made jeep with clothing, blankets, medicine, and
food.

"Hey, you jive honkey mo'fo'!" I spun to find
my assailant, but saw only laughing Creoles. The
only one who wasn't laughing was a powerfully
built man with shiny black skin and wavy hair.
He finally cracked, too, since it was such a good
joke. I was confused, because I know urban black
dialect from my years of living in the Washington,
D.C., area, and I didn't see anyone who looked
like one of "the brothers" standing there.

Marcantonio couldn't bear the suspense and
laughingly told me the big Creole, Carlito, was
my tormentor. A native Nicaraguan, he had gone
to work in the U.S. in his youth and had returned
with a perfect impersonation of the speech of the
blacks he assembled cars with in Detroit. His
friends thought this the funniest thing in the
world, so Carlito never forgot the routine.

We crossed the mountainous central part of
Costa Rica and made our way to the camp on the
humid coastal plain. Central American travelers
on beaten paths grow accustomed to seeing hazy
outlines of nearby ridges through frames of en-
croaching vegetation. But the mountains aren't
like that. The Cordillera de Guanacaste is the
spine of Costa Rica. At eleven thousand feet it
seems more like Andean Peru than Central America. Suddenly the air is cool and soft. Daytime
temperatures sometimes hover in the fifties during the rainy winter.

You see Indians on foot and horseback, carrying the area's produce from one village to another. Lush banana groves and tiny fields of coffee bushes decorate the lower slopes of soaring ridges. Everything that looks murky and distant and gray-green at a lower altitude is sharp and close and emerald. But around the next bend in the road might be a low-lying cloud and visibility can instantly be reduced to a few feet. The contrasts were exhilarating, especially since the traffic was usually heavy with huge eighteen-wheelers making the trek from capital to coast.

The winding road finally took us back down to the other side of the mountains. The humidity was even more oppressive by contrast with the mountain air. But it was like going home for me. Grassy, swampy plains populated by mean-looking tropical cattle. It could have been central Florida instead of Central America. Limón, the port city, was very Caribbean: blacks, palm trees, and lots of laughter and flirting between men and women. We had lunch at a seaside restaurant and dance hall, feasting on delicious *tortuga*—turtle—prepared by fat, black matrons with handkerchiefs on their heads. The minute I saw those women in the kitchen, I was reminded of the South of my youth. I knew the food would be good.

After lunch our first stop was to a safe house of the Creole resistance group who fought alongside Brooklyn Rivera's *Misurasata*. As with all the Nicaraguan fighters I met, these men greeted me warmly. They were enthused that a foreigner was willing to join their cause and fight the common enemy. We had much to talk about.

But Marcantonio and Carlito wanted to get to the refugee camps, so we took off across the coastal plains. My companions good-naturedly hooted at girls walking alongside the road and yelled, "Ooh, la, la!" Costa Rican women are known for their beauty, and my friends nearly fell out of the speeding jeep if one waved back. Carlito laughed with sheer enjoyment and beat the back of the seat with his fist till my neck hurt. When we hadn't seen a girl for a few minutes, I asked the big Creole why so many Nicaraguan refugees on this side of Costa Rica spoke English.

"Most Nicaraguans only speak Spanish," he laughed. "The Latinos. It's mostly just the Indians and us *criollos* that speak English. English-owned black slaves from Jamaica were brought to this coast to work the plantations and lumber mills. They mixed with the Miskitos very easily. The slaves spoke English, of course, and the Indians picked it up from them. You're really better off with English around here. That way they don't think you're Spanish, although with your red hair and beard, there's no way you'll be taken for anything but a gringo, John."

The refugee camps we visited housed several hundred Miskito Indians, mostly refugees from the town of Setnet Point on the Atlantic coast of southern Nicaragua. While Carlito distributed the items we had brought Marcantonio and I spoke with the leader of the young men of the camp, a rangy fellow named Victor. He told us a story that I had heard previously about a Miskito family captured by the Sandinistas while trying to escape being herded into a "relocation camp." The EPS soldiers allegedly had buried this family alive on the beach of Setnet Point. What the Indians did to the Sandinistas they captured after that incident might be described by some as an "atrocity." To others it might be considered payback.

Victor told me the story. Two young Miskito boys set out one night, deliberately walking into a restricted area near the beach. When they were spotted by the Sandinista soldiers patrolling the beach, they broke into a run, leading the patrol into a classic ambush. Every male in the village of Setnet Point awaited the Sandinistas. They were armed with single-shot shotguns, .22-caliber rifles, clubs, and machetes.

The first volley killed most of the soldiers and three dazed and frightened survivors were quickly captured. The prisoners stood trembling in a torchlit circle of Indians, waiting for their fate. If they had known what was in store for them, they never would have surrendered.

The circle broke to permit a short, leather-skinned elder to enter. He walked to within a foot of the Latino soldiers and looked at each one's face in turn. They twitched and fidgeted before his impassive gaze.

"Do you remember me?" he asked them in a quiet, monotonic voice. "I am the preacher that your Sandinista officials do not allow to preach. And I am the judge of this village, but they no longer allow me to settle the disputes among the people of Setnet Point. But I tell you that to-night I will preach to the Indians here, and I will judge, also. I will judge you."

As one, the three Sandinistas tried to bolt through the circle of Miskitos. They were stopped by a wall of sinew and steel.

"Do not struggle. It is useless," the old man continued, the faintest trace of the upward lilt of the Caribbean in his voice. "You have made your-selves our enemy and you will meet your fate to-night. God, Himself, has delivered you into our hands. Therefore, it is useless to struggle," he concluded with quiet logic.

"We had no quarrel with the new government in the west. But you came with the Cubans and the strange-sounding white men and tried to change our lives and our traditions. When some of our poor people tried to leave, you buried them. You didn't even have the decency to kill them like warriors, even though you wear the uni-forms of soldiers. You are not soldiers; you are not even men." The old man spat on the ground in front of the frightened prisoners.

"Now, you will hear your fate. This is my judg-ment. You used your ears to hear the sounds the poor Indians made when they were trying to run away. You will hear no more."

Three muscular Indians stepped up, one be-hind each Sandinista. With all their strength they clapped their cupped hands, one on each side of the soldiers' heads. They screamed in agony as the rush of air pressure into the auricular canals burst their eardrums.

The hapless Sandinistas fell to their knees, moaning and holding their heads. The old Miskito droned on, talking now for the benefit of his people, satisfying their fierce thirst for vengeance and justice. "You used your eyes to see our people when you hunted them down on the beach. You will never see again."

Six bronze hands grabbed each soldier, two on each wrist and two gripping each head in muscular vises. Three more Indians stepped forward. They held sharply pointed sticks that had been heated to a dull, red glow by the fire of the torches. The quiet of the Caribbean night was rent by the piercing, shrill screams of the doomed Sandinistas, as the Miskitos' vengeance claimed their eyes.

The stentorian drone of the old Indian judge continued as if the screams of pain and horror from the doomed wretches didn't exist. "You used your feet to run down our people as if they were rabbits for your stewpot. You will never run again."

Three machetes rose and fell—once, twice—and the three prisoners' screams were reduced to gasps as their central nervous systems rebelled at relaying more impulses from pain sensors. But there was more.

"You used your hands to dig into the sand and make a grave for our brothers and sisters. You will never use your hands against Indians again."

The machetes flashed once, twice more in the

torchlight. By this time the Sandinistas had gone into hemorrhagic shock and were flopping uncontrollably on the ground.

"You have no need of burial. You are not Christians," the old man said. Victor and his friends wiped the blades of their machetes on the uniforms of their dying enemies and followed the elder to the meeting hall. The old Indian preached his last sermon in the village of Setnet Point that night. Victor didn't remember the topic, but a homily from the Book of Exodus would have been appropriate. The entire population fled to sanctuary in Costa Rica the next day.

I had shuddered involuntarily while listening to Victor's unemotional narrative. "This is war," I said to Marcantonio, who had joined us. "This is the real, primal truth of war. Not 'a dispute among nations settled by means other than diplomacy,' as Clausewitz had put it in his classic *On War*, but a war for survival." I thought to myself that when a race, a culture, and certain self-evident truths were at stake, there could be no half-measures in the conflict. I believe I had just learned what every Vietcong cadre must have known.

"You see, John, the Russians place great value on the ports of Nicaragua's Atlantic coast. They are close to Cuba and Grenada, where they have placed great stores of arms earmarked for revolutionaries in Central and South America. Also, the Russians can easily extract the agricultural produce grown in that part of the country. It is loaded on the same ships that bring the arms in and is sent to eastern Europe and the Soviet Union.

"The Indians," he continued, "want to be free to hunt and fish, or loaf if they feel like it. That's their way of life and it has been for centuries. But to the Russians, personal freedom and strategic ports don't go together. They have pressured the Sandinista government into 'relocating' the Indians into camps where they can be strictly controlled. Some say they will eventually be exterminated. I don't know if even the Sandinistas will go that far, but the Indians don't want any part of those camps. They are rebelling all along the coast and giving the Sandinistas fits. Remember the problems your U.S. Cavalry had in trying to implement a similar policy?"

Victor then took me on a tour of the camp, and as I passed the women nursing sickly children, the old men gathered in silent groups, and the children playing with whatever they could find, I was struck with the faces of these Central American Indians. "My God, these people look like Cheyenne or Sioux," I told Marcantonio. The high cheekbones, the shiny black hair, the copper skin, the accented English, even their military tactics . . . it was like being on a reservation in South Dakota.

I watched two four- or five-year-old Indian children playing with some cast-off toys that had been donated to the camp by a Costa Rican church. They weren't very cheerful, but they dutifully ran bright-colored plastic trucks around in the dirt.

At first I thought they'd begun to fight. One of them suddenly plopped back in the dirt. He looked around as if surprised, his face twisted, and he started to cry. Victor told me this happened all the time.

He shouldn't have had to. I had seen the same thing among Vietnamese and Cuban refugee children. Small children . . . and sometimes not-so-small ones . . . who have been taken from their homes, separated from their families, terrorized, underfed, and kept in limbo for too long sometimes just start crying.

There's even a body of psychological literature on the syndrome, as if that somehow legitimizes the problem. It sure makes sense to me. I'd cry too.

Victor and I then met with the young men of the camp who were preparing to leave in two days time for a Misurasata training facility nearby. I tried small talk, but the young Indians had things on their minds.

"The dogs won't let us take our boats out to fish in the sea! Even Somoza didn't mind if we ate."

"Everything was better under Somoza."

"Maybe not everything, but everything that concerned us."

"That's right. We were all right. But here we meet men who suffered under Somoza in the cities, they lost property or were imprisoned. But on the Atlantic coast, Somoza left us alone."

"Yes, others here suffered. But all of you should notice that even they are here, and not in

Nicaragua. Even here in the camp is better than Nicaragua right now."

The young men were angry . . . and ready to fight. And, after this day of listening to them, I was ready to fight for them.

But I would not be allowed to join their ranks. My escorts had orders to return me to San José.

As the road climbed from the coastal plain and into the mountains, I told my companions that I hoped the news from Commander Zero would come soon. I told Marcantonio I was ready to go back to the Creoles and the Indians, if they would just stop the jeep and let me disappear.

"John, you're like William Walker . . . a dreamer. You know him?"

"Is he living down here?"

"My God, no! The Hondurans put him in front of a firing squad back in 1860."

"Well, then, I'm not like him—nobody's going to execute me. But now I know who you're talking about—the gringo who invaded Baja, California."

"The same! Walker is still a hero to many Central American adventurers. He invaded Mexico once and later conquered Nicaragua. And only the collaboration of the U.S. Navy and Nicaragua's neighbors drove him out. Then he tried Honduras. The British captured him and turned him over to the Hondurans. They shot him. He was in his mid-thirties when he died, and had been a doctor, a lawyer, and a newspaperman in your country.

"Another Walker might turn the tide in this

war. Do you think you could be another William Walker?"

"If I'm not, it won't be for lack of effort."

"Then, Mr. William Walker, Jr., you should know the ghost of William Walker is what frightens the Nicaraguans about U.S. intervention in Central America. You will be a very big target. And many of the anti-Sandinistas will not trust you, just because you'll remind them of him. Nicaraguans are great students of history, John."

Everybody *had* treated me with caution, even those with some reason to trust me. Even Marcantonio. But I couldn't be offended. For all they knew, I was KGB or DGI. Of course most of them thought I was a CIA agent. In fact, many of them *hoped* that I was, and that my entry into their organization meant that America was going to more actively assist the Contras of the southern front.

Upon our return to San José I was instructed to meet El Gringo at 2000 hours at the political offices. I would then be escorted to San Pedro, where I would hear the voice of Commander Zero. He would decide my case by radio from his base in the southern front of the war.

Everyone knows about *"manana."* An invitation for dinner at eight in Latin America really means to come by about ten. That's as much a part of their culture and value system as punctuality is of ours.

Well, the military people were different, I found. Precision and timing are universal military virtues, and exactly at eight the security vehicle showed up and I was escorted, along with several armed guards, to the military headquarters in the suburbs of San José.

San Pedro was a heavily guarded compound. It housed not only military headquarters but a supply warehouse and radio facilities with tall antennas bristling and high-powered transmitters humming in the background. It was the heart and nerve center of the military command of the democratic forces on the southern front of Nicaragua.

I cooled my heels and swapped stories with some of the veterans who were on guard duty while radio contact was being made.

"Why are you here?"

Good question, I thought, as I mentally translated my answer into what I hoped was passable Spanish. *"Yo creo en la democracia,"* I answered. *"You amo la libertad, y yo odio el communismo. Yo quiero luchar a favor de las fuerzas democraticas, mis amigos."*

Evidently this was considered a good answer, if not good Spanish, and I was slapped on the back and hands were shaken all around. The vets gave me tips on how to protect my skin against the various insects of the tropical rain forest on the southern front and other helpful, practical hints.

But I never got to hear Pastora on the radio that night. One of the San Pedro staff members came out to where I was waiting and told me that Commander Zero had told him that if I really wanted to help them, I would go back to America and raise money for their cause.

He went on to state that Commandante Pastora had said that no gringo could ever fight for his forces.

This didn't sit too well with me, but there was no one to argue with. So I left and plotted my next move in joining this war.

While I had been working with the people of the Democratic Alliance, I had also made contact —thanks to Marcantonio, with whom I had developed a real friendship—with some of the other anti-Sandinista groups headquartered in San José. Among these were the Committee for Human Rights, headed by Jose Esteban Gonzales, and the UDN of Negro Chamorro, which had pulled out of the Alliance. I had not only gotten to meet El Negro, himself, but his son-in-law, Norman, had become one of my drinking buddies in San José's plentiful watering spots.

Based on the recommendations of several members of the human-rights group, I had been well received by El Negro's people and had also made contact with their military branch. El Negro's adjutant, Carlos, told me that if Pastora did not want me as a combatant, they certainly did, and that in three days time they would fly me to their CIA-sponsored camp in Honduras. I would go into battle with the forces of El Negro, if not with Commander Zero.

El Negro was one of the heroes of the war against Somoza and the first leader to break with the Sandinista government after their Marxist orientation was revealed. He's a popular, charismatic man in his fifties, but robust and fearless.

Unlike Pastora, Chamorro actually led his troops into combat.

Meanwhile, Cesar Aviles contacted me to say that he and Robelo were angry that I had not been accepted into the Contra forces as promised, and that they would take steps to ensure that I could join the fighting on their side. Aviles managed to do this in a very clever way. He drove me down to their recruiting office and had me signed up as an ordinary recruit.

On August 20, 1983, I filled out enlistment papers, took the oath, was issued a set of dog tags bearing the number 1486, and told I would be contacted when the next convoy was headed to the front. So I was now on the verge of being in two armies simultaneously. At least they were fighting the same enemy—the Sandinistas. I went back to my rented *finca*, packed my gear, stood by, and sure enough the next night I got a call saying "Let's go."

CHAPTER SEVEN

REENLISTMENT

I found myself in the back of a Toyota jeep with five other Contras. Ryan was a Vietnam veteran of a combat engineer battalion who had lived in the United States for ten or twelve years. He had returned to help free his country from the Communist menace.

There was Santiago, a former sergeant in the Guardia Nacional of General Somoza. He had been shot in the right elbow by an FAL during the last war and his scars gave strong evidence to the efficacy of 7.62-mm NATO ball ammunition. He had been flown, like many of the other Guardia Nacional casualties, to Miami and treated at Baptist Hospital. The bill was paid by General Anastasio Somoza.

Santiago stayed in the United States and was working at a cattle ranch near Okeechobee, Florida, when he was contacted by Contra recruiting agents from Miami. He jumped at the chance to join the fight against his former enemies. Santiago became my friend and one of the best NCO's I've known in a military career spanning three conflicts on as many continents.

Another fellow sharing the jolting ride with us in the back of the jeep was El Aguila, the Eagle. He was the best cook I came across in all of Central America. Aguila could make rice and beans taste good after you'd been eating it and little else for weeks. He was twenty-nine years old and a *campesino*. I asked him why he had joined the Contra army.

"I've been a *campesino* all my life, Dr. John," he told me. "I don't want to be stuck in the fields forever. In your country few people work in the earth with their hands. But under Sandinismo many dig and plant and harvest by hand because the fools don't know how to run the economy. I want to be something different . . . something more than a peasant. I'm tired of digging with a shovel and chopping with a machete. If we succeed in winning a democratic victory, I will have my chance to be more in life than a *campesino*."

Carlos, a Cuban from Miami, was also with us. Tall, pale, and shifty-eyed, I took an instant dislike to him. He said little on the trip, but grew more and more nervous as we neared our destination. I asked him if he was a *combatiente*.

No," he replied. *"Intelligencia."*

Uh-huh, I thought. *I'll just bet you are, Cubano, but for which side?*

Bolivar, a short, jovial, round-faced little fellow from Managua, sat next to me and regaled us with tales of his sexual prowess, recently demon-

strated, he claimed, on a week of R and R in San
José.

Up front was our driver, Chempena. He could
easily have qualified as a champion demolition-
derby driver if he had ever chosen to come to
America.

Also in the front of the Toyota were two
women. One, Maria, had been a member of the
Sandinista security agency and was going back
into Nicaragua as a double agent on behalf of the
Contras. Next to her was Elena, who was working
as a combat nurse, although her training had only
been as a nurse's aide. Even the minimal skills she
possessed were far superior to the first aid practiced by the average Nicaraguan combatant and
she was vitally needed.

We drove through the rainy night on the twist-
ing, mountainous roads until we reached the town
of Boca San Carlos, where the road turned into a
bumpy trail. We followed this trail some twenty
kilometers into the jungle until it dissolved into a
sea of mud that mired our Toyota jeep above the
axles.

We unloaded our personal gear and hiked
through the darkness to an outpost where we
made camp for what remained of the night.

I then had my introduction to Nicaraguan
mosquitoes. They loved my Cutter's brand of insect repellent. The call must have gone out all
over southern Nicaragua for the local mosquitoes
to come sample the new gringo delicacy—
namely, me and my Cutters. This brand was later
discarded in favor of Deep Wood's OFF, pre-

ferred in large spray cans by all of Pastora's *guerrilleros*.

We found hammocks rolled up at the outpost, tied them to nearby trees, and slept until dawn. At first light we rose, washed in the clear, cool water of a mountain stream, and hiked back to the jeep. It was an hour's muddy march down the road to pick up the cargo that we had left in the locked vehicle. Our progress was slow due to the large loads we were carrying on the return trip and I had time to observe the beauty of the triple-canopy rain forest.

Kongos trooped through the second level, just out of sight. Flowers fell in chains, and lace collars of moss and ferns decorated bases of giant trees. The *kongos* tracked us as we walked and finally moved close enough that we could see them. The Nicaraguans laughed at the monkeys, and their mutual antics made the mud easier to take.

When we returned to the outpost, we were met by Israel and El Brazo. This guy looked like he'd spent his life in a weight-lifting room. Many Central Americans are tough, but you don't see a lot of muscle bulk. El Brazo looked like a brown Mr. T, with a thicker, shorter neck.

"*Hola*, Bolivar! Did you see her again? Is she still old, or did the whiskey make her look young again?" El Brazo played rough, but Bolivar didn't mind. The Contras in this camp hadn't seen a woman in a month, and he had.

Banter paved the path to the camp. Then we had to spend twenty minutes making sure everybody shook hands with everybody else. Central Americans shake hands a lot, but it's almost a national pastime with the Nicas.

They escorted us to a farm on the Costa Rican side of the Rio San Juan. This farm was owned by a fellow called Shorty. He was an interesting individual, a wealthy Costa Rican with extensive holdings along the border and a fine, large house in San José. Shorty was also a *combatiente* and platoon leader for the Contra forces. Luis, Shorty's foreman, treated us to healthy portions of rice and beans immediately upon our arrival at the farm. Then he raised Pastora on the radio and told him that replacements had arrived.

Uh-oh, I thought. *Pastora is going to learn that I'm here, become angry, and order me shot, or perhaps, worse yet, sent back to civilian life.*

He was told that there was a nurse among the replacements.

"Bueno!" Pastora said. "Send her in immediately."

Another exchange followed on the radio, and a voice confirmed that a canoe was being dispatched right away from Camp TPH. They had suffered casualties during a recent action.

Luis then told Commander Zero that a doctor was included among the replacements.

"Bueno! Send the doctor up also."

"No, no, Commandante. He is a *psicologo*, a head doctor," the radio operator told him.

"Bueno! There are some people here I want him to talk to."

Everyone in the farmhouse chuckled at this display of Pastora's wit. I felt relief and dared to hope that I had finally arrived at the war I had been seeking.

Whether Pastora had forgotten about the transmission from San Pedro a few nights previously, or whether he thought to himself, *If this gringo wants to join my army so badly, I'll humor him*, I'll probably never know. However, he not only accepted me into his service, but ordered the supply sergeant to issue me brand-new U.S. Army equipment and the Belgian-made FN FAL rather than the surplus gear and ancient AK-47s being passed out to the other replacements.

Shorty's farm was a working farm—complete with livestock, outbuildings, cultivated fields, and crops. But when it was time for the equipment to be issued, floors opened up and rucksacks and web gear were pulled out of their hidden compartments. On the wall of a side room hung saddles and other tack, concealing the lever that, when pulled, opened up one wall to reveal stacks of camouflage fatigues, jungle boots, and other military gear. We then went to the barn and climbed up to the loft, which housed a corncrib. The corn was shoveled aside and the floor raised to expose an impressive pile of AK-47s, FALs, and even some old M1 Garands.

"Why is the gringo getting new equipment and an FAL while I have this rusty Kalashnikov?" queried Aguila.

Luis snapped, "Because he'll put it to better use."

That was the first and only sign of animosity among any of the Contras I saw during my Central American odyssey.

CHAPTER EIGHT

NICARAGUA REVISITED

We traveled from Shorty's farm up the Rio San Juan by dugout canoe to a camp known as Z-3. This camp consisted of one thatched-roof hut that had been the residence of the chief of the Guardia Frontera, but I was told that he no longer needed this residence or any other this side of hell. The bullet holes in the walls and the craters in the clearing around the hut answered any further questions about the fate of the previous occupants.

Santiago, Aguila, Bolivar, and I settled down into this camp, unpacked our gear, hung our hammocks, and divided security duties. We organized a training regimen that included patrolling, marksmanship, survival tactics, and for me an introduction to camp life and soldiering *"a lo Nicaragüense."* This included fishing in the Rio San Juan and—until I learned that the freshwater sharks were man-eaters—bathing and swimming in it. Z-3 was a primitive camp, but the surrounding jungle was rich in animal and plant life, which

made our lives much more bearable in the steaming heat of the Central American rainy season.
The diet was rich and varied: fresh fish from the
nearby river and streams, an occasional arma-
dillo, all the rice and beans you could stand,
quantities of canned meat and tuna. Nearby grew
oranges, grapefruit, bananas, plantains, and even
a few pineapples.

As I breakfasted that first morning in Z-3 on
slices of pineapple, fresh-squeezed orange juice,
and eggs provided by a friendly farmer, I thought
to myself that this was not going to be such a bad
war after all. At least the chow was good.

"Quieres cafe, John?"

"Si, mil gracias, companero," I told Aguila.

"Norteamericanos like their coffee without
leche," Santiago told the others. "They call it
'coffee black.'"

"Ha ha. John, *tu quieres* 'coffee black'? Ha ha
ha ha."

Those were just about the only two words of
English that Aguila ever learned and he found
them hilarious.

"They also drink their orange juice *crudo,"*
Santiago continued. The others were incredulous.
Nicaraguans drink their breakfast juice diluted
with water and sweetened with ample quantities
of sugar. I don't know if they considered our
habit to be a gauche display of conspicuous con-
sumption or evidence that the yanquis were really barbarians after all.

Santiago, Aguila, and I became fast friends.
They showed me where to find edible plants and

which ones should be avoided. Daily we patrolled our area of responsibility, searching for signs of enemy activity, checking our trip wires and booby traps, and harvesting the offerings of the jungle.

They were such good foragers that we often radioed other camps to report surpluses of fruit. Canoes would arrive, paddled by dark-eyed, heavily armed *companeros*, to pick up a stalk of bananas or a bag of oranges. The generosity of the Nicaraguans was overwhelming. El Tigre, commander of Camp TPH, had been given a side of beef by a collaborator in his zone. After feeding his men he radioed each camp for a head count, portioned out the remainder, and personally delivered it to each camp in his and the neighboring zones. Each man's share of this windfall was one ounce.

I had never seen such sharing, even in American fighting men. *God, I love these guys,* I told myself. I was prepared to die to restore Nicaragua to such people.

Beauty was mainly what I saw in the jungle. But those who think only of the beauty have never lived in the jungle. Those curtains of green are filled with thorns that cause blood poisoning, poisonous caterpillars, vines that grab your legs and gear, snakes whose venom kills in twenty minutes, and every jungle animal with a voice screams as if to wake the dead and drive them mad.

But the rain is still worse. Gringos who have

seen the fall rains of the South or the month-long drizzles of Seattle really don't know what wet is. Rain in Central America sounds like a freight train as wind whips giant tropical trees, whistles through vines, and the solid strata of falling water beats everything movable to the fungus-roped earth. You can't see, can't hear, can't move. All you can do is hide.

And the water brings mold. Like death, fungus finally conquers everything else in the jungle. Gringos smell it from the moment they get off the plane, but the natives don't even know what you're talking about. And in a wet, hot country it doesn't just eat your web gear and anything made of leather, it attacks your living body. Every man who has lived in the jungle has a skin stained from fungal infections.

But mud is still the worst thing. Mud up to your ankles does something to make life seem like one long, bad dream. A tired, demoralized man could die of dehydration because he dreaded the fatigue of a two-hundred-meter walk for water.

The training days stretched into weeks, with no action or contact with the Sandinista forces, and I grew restless. But one morning while on patrol several kilometers north of our camp, Aguila, Santiago, and I found a hut at the edge of a stream. We skirted its perimeter, our eyes searching constantly for any sign of movement or life. We covered each other and moved quickly but silently through the brush, closer and closer to the house. Even though it seemed to be vacant, we rushed it with rifles at the ready and burst through the open doorway. What we found was an abandoned cache for either the EPS or the Frontier Guards. The hut contained several cases of canned sardines and some moldy bags of rice.

But our biggest find was a stack of AK-47 ammunition in boxes with Arabic writing on them. I had been told by Marcantonio that all the PLO terrorists who had been evacuated from Beirut after the Israeli incursion into Lebanon and had been shipped to Tripoli were immediately sent on to Nicaragua by Colonel Kadhafi. Evidently he did not want a large number of armed foreigners in his country and sent them on to Nicaragua as an act of solidarity with his Marxist Sandinista brothers. The ammunition was evidence that Marcantonio knew what he was talking about. We filled our packs with the rations and ammo and struggled through the jungle back to Z-3, humping like pack animals.

Santiago took point and cautioned against any unnecessary noise.

We made a mistake. Because we were carrying an immense load, with all the ammunition and cans in our packs, we headed back for Z-3 by the most direct route, which was the way we had come. You *never* go back the same way you came out on a patrol. As we neared a place on the trail where the stream on our left and the jungle on our right squeezed together to form a narrow passage, a hornet landed on my bare right arm and sank its stinger deep into the muscle. The pain from the tiny insect's toxin was severe. It was like a red-hot needle had been thrust into the bicep. I bit my lip in the effort to keep silent and flicked the hostile insect off with my left hand. Just as I was congratulating myself on having maintained noise discipline in spite of this provocation, a shot rang out and clipped hairs from my left arm.

"SON-OF-A-BITCH!" I cried, and hit the ground.

"*HIJO DE LA GRAN PUTA!*" My curse was echoed by Aguila.

Santiago, in front of me, opened up on full auto, his AK raking the jungle ahead of us. Aguila pivoted and dropped to the ground, covering our rear with his assault rifle. I lay in the center of our three-man patrol wanting to scan the jungle for a sign of our unseen enemy, yet at the same time not wanting to raise my head and perhaps get more than a few hairs clipped. Santiago crawled off the trail into the jungle. He reappeared some ten minutes later and waved us forward. Our unseen ambushers had fled without a trace.

Well, I thought. That wasn't much, but it certainly was contact. Best of all, I was still alive.

During our stay at Z-3 we had periodic visitors from other camps, some of whom came just to look at the gringo, I'm sure. Other visitors had different motives.

One day while my *companeros* were out on a training patrol, an Indian paddled his dugout up to the bamboo dock that Santiago and I had built. With the Indian was a tall white man. His steel-gray crew-cut hair and erect posture said "military." I greeted him with the customary handshakes and asked his business at Z-3. The visitor said that he wanted to see Pastora.

I shrugged and told him that Pastora hadn't been around. He asked if I could raise him by radio. I answered that I would have to know who he was and what his business was before I could send a coded message to Camp Tango. "Besides that," I continued, picking up my FAL. "I want to know what you're doing in a war zone."

After some hesitation, interspersed with hemming and hawing, he told me that he was a colonel in the United States Army.

"Southern Command?" I asked.

"No. Adjutant General's Office," was the curt reply.

Jesus! I wondered silently. Pentagon. What's the fucking Pentagon doing at a guerrilla base camp in the jungles of Nicaragua?

I coded the message and radioed Tango. Tadeo, the camp commander, confirmed that the message had been received and understood.

"Colonel, I suggest you and your guide wait at Don Eduardo's *finca* on the Costa Rican side of the river. I'll patch any response through to you when Tango gets back to me."

He nodded agreement and headed to the canoe. I snapped to attention and threw him a crisp salute.

He shook his head. "I'm not really here," he said, and handed me a business card. "But if you get down to San José, call me."

Tadeo radioed later that day, saying that he would send a power launch to pick up the gringo colonel and that I should forget the incident.

Near the end of August I was taken by Pastora's son, Ernesto, to visit Camp Tango, where I met Commandante Tadeo, Steve Salisbury, a correspondent from *Soldier of Fortune* magazine in the United States, and a host of veteran *querrilleros.* I was peppered with questions from Tadeo's men:

"Are you in the U.S. Army?"

"Are you a Green Beret?"

"Are there more Americans coming?"

"Will the U.S. Marines be here soon to help us?"

Some of the less verbal fighters sat and stared at me with those stolid, impassive Indian eyes that never seem to blink. I remember thinking that some of these men probably had never seen a gringo in their lives. The overall impression that I got was that these men, mainly Nicaraguan peasants and Panamanian volunteers, regarded my arrival as an extremely positive sign. I felt really welcome when one of them offered me part of his rations.

I went inside the headquarters building at Tango, an aging ramshackle farmhouse, and conferred with Tadeo regarding the training of his men and the use of some Chinese-made recoilless rifles that had recently been obtained from Israeli sources.

"You will help us learn to fire these things, and I will give you a Browning machine gun so that you can kill many *piricuacos.*" *Piricuaco* is a term meaning rabid dog in Nicaraguan slang and that's what all Contras called the Sandinistas. The Sandinistas called us Somocistas and sons-of-bitches and often talked about our mothers.

When I left Tadeo's HQ and walked through the group of *guerrilleros,* I noted with a smile that the subject of intense debate was whether their cause would be better served by the intervention of U.S. Marines or by Special Forces.

CHAPTER NINE

THE GLORY OF WAR

Combat has been described as moments of terror broken up by hours and days of boredom. I don't know what army the joker was in who coined that phrase, but in my experience those moments of terror have been broken up by hours, days, and even weeks of hard work. The war against the Sandinistas was no exception.

We had finally acquired a helicopter and Commander Zero planned to use it to haul in supplies and evacuate casualties. This was to be an important first for our forces, because medevacs were nonexistent up to that point. If you caught a bullet in the Nicaraguan jungles, you could usually kiss your ass good-bye long before any medical treatment could be reached.

Pastora was planning an attack against the ancient citadel at El Castillo. Four hundred Sandinista troops were occupying this town on the Rio San Juan and were headquartered in a fortress that had been attacked two centuries ago by English pirates under the command of Henry

Morgan. The *piricuacos* at El Castillo interfered with Pastora's plan to control the southern border between Costa Rica and Nicaragua and had been targeted for an attack by the entire combined forces of the democratic exile groups in the south. At that time the Sandinistas had few helicopters in the south, and we could just about count on no reinforcements getting to El Castillo from their large base at San Carlos or the smaller line camps scattered along the front.

Patrols increased in both frequency and size as more and more freedom fighters gathered at Camp Tango, arriving aboard a motley collection of jungle craft. Contact with the enemy increased, as did the tempo of activity along the border river. Antique artillery pieces were brought in by dugout canoe and bamboo rafts; four-wheel-drive vehicles struggled through the mud to convoy supplies and reinforcements from headquarters in San José; spies and double agents infiltrated and ex-filtrated across the border, and recon patrols probed the Sandinista defenses daily.

Waiting for action, I drew an assignment. I was ordered to accompany a detail to a secret location within fifteen kilometers of El Castillo. The mission: Construct a *helipuerto* that would give Pastora's forces their first medevac capability. We called it "Operation Falcon."

We saddled up at Z-3 and set out by dugout canoe. The officer in charge was my old friend Shorty, the wealthy Costa Rican whose love of freedom had led him to join this war on behalf of his Nicaraguan cousins. Shorty was small in stature but long on courage and ability. His son accompanied us, along with four tough veteran Nicaraguan *guerrilleros*. Shorty and I carried the Belgian-made FN FALs, as did most of Pastora's officers. The others were armed with Soviet AK-47s.

We left our canoe about five kilometers from our objective and set out on foot. Our guide, Luis, returned to Z-3 to await our radioed pickup order. The trail wound through typical Nicaraguan jungle. War in a *National Geographic* special, I thought as we hiked through the dense jungle.

Birds sang and the air was liquid with the perfume of flowers mixed with the inescapable jungle odor, like living in a wet steamer trunk. The march was almost pleasant. Then the point man —a Miskito Indian—gestured toward the footprints of a Sandinista patrol that had used the same trail within the last day or two. The party was over—lock and load.

As we got farther from the river the trail dried somewhat and we were able to move rapidly. A few hours fast walk brought us to a jungle clearing near a tributary of the San Juan. It would be a bad place to work, but these map coordinates represented the first possible stop in the downhill run from El Castillo. This is where we needed the pad if we were going to resupply retreating troops and evacuate wounded. And our superiors expected to be able to put a chopper here.

We were beat and our task seemed all but impossible, but like good soldiers since the days of Alexander the Great, we made camp. Since this would be home for some time, we spent the rest of that day setting and pitching our tentlike *champas*—squares of plastic material spread across a vine tied lengthwise above our hammocks. We cut fields of fire, assigned security duties, and reconnoitered the area. We had to be ready if the *piricuacos* found us. We were ready for sleep by the time the hot tropical night fell.

Dawn was our signal to wake, and reveille was played by soldiers' quiet laughter and grumbles. Breakfast was good, just like dinner: rice, beans, and strong coffee. It was time to take stock, plan our work, and begin.

Our basic materials were seven strong men, seven machetes, one chain saw, and a jig to hold the chain saw and a log, so we could cut rough lumber from fallen trees. Our construction materials were those offered by the jungle. And the arena for our struggle was a hundred-yard-diameter jungle clearing surrounded by triple-canopy jungle and carpeted in five feet of wiry jungle scrub.

Some might expect helicopters to land in such a place, but they can't. Rotary-wing aircraft—helicopters—do not perform miracles. They're just machines. They differ from conventional, or fixed-wing, aircraft only in that they are more complicated, harder to fly, tend to fall rather than glide when anything goes wrong, and they make bigger messes when they crash at a given speed.

Yet, I've seen choppers snatch wounded from mountaintops, land in an area the size of their blade sweep, and take off and fly away while being riddled with ground fire. But you don't fly that way every day if you expect to live long. For a chopper to fly reliably and safely it needs a solid, well-marked landing pad and cleared entry and exit avenues. That's the sort of thing the Seabees and the Army Corps of Engineers do with bulldozers. We did it with hand tools.

Work started with a skirmish line of *guerrilleros* wielding machetes. Slashing and piling brush, we leveled the clearing to stubble over the soft, waterlogged earth in a few hours. From the beginning we had known the mud wouldn't hold a loaded helicopter. That's why we'd brought the chain saw.

We staked an area for the pad and then walked into the jungle to choose trees for pilings. Thirteen straight hardwood trees with boles over a foot in diameter were felled, limbed, and cut to eight-foot lengths. Then we carried them to the staked area.

While some men cut and carried pilings the rest of us dug holes. Each hole was five feet deep, leaving three feet of piling exposed as a leg for the landing platform. Combat engineers in a modern army would have brought out an auger on a backhoe. Our method was simpler and user-tested for over twenty thousand years.

We cut saplings about six feet long and sliced the ends off at a sharp angle. Archaeologists call this a digging stick and tell us that the cave dwellers used such implements. Nicaraguan peasants are often too poor to afford steel shovels, so they still use digging sticks. It's backbreaking labor in the strictest sense. But Nicaraguans do not complain. It's a way of life to them.

The pilings were set into holes and dirt tamped in around them with the square end of the digging stick until they were solidly planted in the damp jungle earth. El Brazo leveled the tops of the pilings with the same effective simplicity. He cut two stakes three feet long, tied a string between them, and stretched it over the planted pilings. The muscular Nicaraguan then trimmed them with his machete, his keen eye ensuring near perfection.

Shorty and his son set up the jig for their chain saw. Then they fed felled trees into the make-do lumber mill, producing straight, square-edged, hardwood, two-by-six-inch, sixteen-foot-long planks and solid four-by-four timbers. Looking at all that clean, straight, fresh lumber where there had been nothing but brush made me feel like we could do anything.

The rest of us began to clear more trees from the entrance and exit sallies. Five of us cut down a total of two hundred trees in less than two days using nothing but machetes. Trunks ranged from two inches to two feet in diameter and cutting them required a sharp blade. A lesson I learned on this mission was to keep a file handy to renew the machete's edge every half hour or so. Nine years of university study had not furnished me with such practical knowledge.

By the time we had hacked out our little airport's takeoff and landing corridors, the Costa Rican father and son team had finished milling the lumber. We made a frame of four-by-fours on top of the pilings, and then nailed the heavy two-by-six planks to make a deck for the helipad.

Less than seventy-two hours after we had left Z-3, the coded message went out: "Mission accomplished." Operation Falcon was coming in. We camouflaged the pad, broke camp, and hiked to our rendezvous with Luis, secure in the knowledge that when needed the chopper could resupply us and evacuate our casualties.

After our return to Z-3 I treated my blistered feet and rested in my hammock, enjoying the pleasant ache that comes from having accomplished something difficult yet worthwhile.

CHAPTER TEN

COMMANDER ZERO

Finally, the great day arrived.

Toward the end of the first week of September 1983, Pastora himself—the almost legendary Commander Zero—strode into our camp like a bantam rooster, sporting a Castro-type beard and wearing a fatigue cap emblazoned with a red star. His handpicked body guard set up a defensive perimeter and maintained a high state of alert while he inspected our small unit.

Pastora had boasted that his was a true "people's army": no rank, few insignia, no ceremony. But when I presented myself and threw him a sharp salute, he drew himself up to attention and returned it just as crisply.

"*A sus ordenes, Commandante,*" I barked.

"*Correcto,*" he replied.

He cautioned me to speak to him only in Spanish, and inquired into my military background and specialties. He grunted approval when I mentioned reconnaissance and combat intelligence. Pastora then announced that I would not join the

raid on El Castillo. Instead I would join his staff
and help him prepare tactical plans for small-unit
actions and ambush patrols to precede and follow
the main attack.

What I didn't know at the time was that Pastora constantly changed his mind. In fact, it was
a joke among the soldiers. We prepared many tactical plans regarding this upcoming attack on El
Castillo, all of which were enthusiastically approved by Pastora but never implemented. The
next day he would ask for new plans or come up
with a totally different idea. As a feeling of exas-
peration began to overcome my dedication to
these assigned duties, a minor disaster struck.

Costa Rican security forces had been harassing
the Contras for some time. They had seized ship-
ments of supplies, arrested our people on various
pretexts, and raided training camps inside Costa
Rica. A particularly important shipment, including mortars, machine guns, and medical supplies,
had been confiscated as they were being unloaded
from a freighter off the port city of Limón one
moonless night.

Pastora headed south to try to put an end to
the harassment. He had decided on direct action:
He would steal the stuff back, sending his elite
squad of bodyguards into the customs warehouse
where the goods were stored. Pastora sent the
bodyguards south in civilian clothing and the rest
of the staff to Tango.

I was told to supervise the tearing down of the
radio station and the evacuation of the troops
and equipment from Z-3 and to wait on the river

for further orders. In the midst of this feverish activity I visited briefly with Don Eduardo, owner of the large ranch on the Costa Rican side of the river directly across from Z-3. The rancher was a Contra collaborator and had graciously hosted Commander Zero during his visit to our zone. Don Eduardo had a young wife and a son and was the proud owner of over three hundred head of cattle. He was the local *patron* and played that role to the hilt.

I asked him why the Costa Rican authorities were giving the Contras such grief, since Costa Rica was supposed to be a democracy. In my naiveté I assumed that all democratic countries would be willing to help anti-Communist movements, especially when the Communist country was a neighbor and a potential threat to their own security.

Don Eduardo replied that the Costa Rican government was between a rock and a hard place. Costa Rica has a small but hard-core Communist Party and its government contains many Communist sympathizers and others of strong left-wing political persuasion. Besides, he told me, during the last war against Somoza, Costa Rica had overtly aided the Sandinistas by allowing them to maintain unmolested camps on the Costa Rican side of the border. From these they raided into General Somoza's strongholds.

These ties with the Sandinistas carried on now that they were the ruling power in Nicaragua even though they had openly avowed their Marxism.

"But," I protested, "the people of Costa Rica are obviously in favor of the democratic forces."

He smiled at me rather condescendingly and asked me if my government always reflected the will of its people.

I thanked Don Eduardo for the information and returned to the supervision of the work going on at Z-3. When the last boat left I was alone.

Two days went by with no contact from anyone and I began to feel that I had been abandoned. Disgusted, I left my rifle and other gear with a family of Indian collaborators whose farmhouse served as a supply depot, packed up my personal gear, my Colt .45 and three hand grenades, and set out to walk the thirty kilometers out of the jungle to the town of Boca San Carlos.

The Sandinistas sometimes raided into Costa Rica to kidnap and murder Contra collaborators, and Costa Rican security forces had arrested our fighters found on the wrong side of the border. I vowed not to be captured by the Sandinistas or arrested by the Costa Rican Civil Guard.

Speed was essential to my safety. I couldn't afford to linger, and an overnight camp would represent unnecessary exposure, but I had to get out of Nicaragua. I put the .45 and the grenades on my web belt, shouldered a burlap bag stuffed with seventy pounds of gear, and began a race with the dark. Munching rice balls from my pockets, pausing only to drink untreated water from streams as I crossed them, and to wash my feet in puddles and change socks, I carried a load of nearly half my own weight through twenty miles of heavy jungle.

Exhausted, I reached a village near Boca San Carlos seven and one half hours after I'd set out. I hired a car and driver to take me to San José. As soon as I reached the city I reported to headquarters at San Pedro. Pastora said with a groan that he had forgotten he left me on the river. All twelve of his bodyguards were incarcerated in a Costa Rican jail because his inept plot to burglarize the customs house had fallen through.

That was the last straw. Missions had been planned and aborted or simply forgotten. Pastora's plans rarely ever proved effective in execution. Finally, Pastora had twice postponed the attack on El Castillo because he had press interviews. Obviously press contact was more important to this "hero" than contact with the enemy.

I couldn't fight a war that way. I requested a transfer to a more active unit. The request was granted.

CHAPTER ELEVEN

R AND R

Before reporting for the new assignment, I decided to enjoy a brief rest and recreation with my wife. She had cleaned out the house in Florida, sold the cars, the boat, and the appliances and come to Costa Rica.

I met her at the Juan Santamaria International Airport and drove her to the ranch I'd rented. It was nestled high in the mountains northeast of San José and was often above the clouds. On clear nights the sparkling lights of the capital seemed to merge with the panorama of stars winking and shimmering in the black sky. The view, when there was one, was never less than magnificent.

For four hundred dollars a month I'd signed a lease on an American-style ranch house, furnished comfortably, along with six Doberman pinschers thrown in for security. A handyman and the use of a saddle horse were included in the rental price and the handyman's wife was available for housecleaning at a hundred *colones* a day, about two dollars and a quarter in American money. I thought this relative luxury would ease the culture shock for Alex.

We toured Costa Rica like typical vacationers, except that our itinerary included refugee camps. I wanted her to see why I was fighting for the Contras. She saw and understood. When we returned to San José she, too, paid a visit to the democratic alliance recruiting office and enlisted as a nurse.

"What is your pseudonym?" *Nacho*, the recruiting officer, asked her.

"My what?" Alexandra replied.

I explained to her that the Nicaraguans who had families still in Nicaragua used pseudonyms to protect their loved ones from retaliation from the Sandinistas if it became known that they were fighting with the Contras. She asked me if I had a pseudonym.

"Dr. John," I replied.

"That makes sense," she said. "You're a doctor and your name is John. Call me 'Alejandra,'" she told the recruiter.

She was assigned to a pediatric clinic that served the exile community's children.

While she was filling out the extensive history required by security, I phoned the mysterious colonel. He was leaving for the States the next day and wanted to see me immediately. I gave him the address of a cafe operated by trustworthy Nicaraguan friends and told him we could meet in thirty minutes.

The colonel seemed nervous. "I understand

you're strictly a free-lancer," he said after introductions.

"Look, Colonel," I snapped back, "I'm an American, and even though, as I'm sure you know by now, I don't work for the United States government, I don't work against it. We checked out the alliance and we're both satisfied that these people's principles are in accord with what we consider the American way."

Alexandra nodded her agreement and proudly displayed her new dog tags. I went on, "Further, it just might be in America's best interests to have someone like me in the democratic alliance both now and after the war."

He chose not to respond to my verbal display of patriotism. "I understand you took some pictures in Managua."

"I thought you'd never ask," I chuckled, and produced the packet of developed photographs I'd smuggled out of Nicaragua. He pocketed them without inspection and rose.

"Next time you come back to San José, give this man a call. He might want to ask you a few questions."

"Well, Alex," I said when he had left, "we're following the game plan. I'll bet anything that he just gave me the number of the CIA station chief in San José."

CHAPTER TWELVE

THE MOON GETS BLOODY

I was sent to a camp called Luna Roja, which literally means "Red Moon." But to the Contra troops it was known as "Bloody Moon." One unit had suffered heavy casualties there a few months before. Luna Roja was four hundred meters inside the "neutral" country of Costa Rica and about fifty kilometers west of El Castillo.

Life at Luna Roja was not like it had been at the Z camps near Pastora's headquarters. I learned many more things about Pastora's army while at Luna Roja, including the fact that the farther a unit was removed physically from Pastora, the less awe he seemed to inspire in the men. And the farther an officer was removed politically from Pastora, the less supplies he received for his men.

At Luna Roja we had sixty men and only seven canteens. There were rucksacks but no straps, equipment belts but no harnesses or suspenders. Men tied ropes, padded with rags, to their packs so they could carry them on their backs. We had weapons but few cleaning kits, and small numbers of mortar rounds, hand grenades, and rockets for the RPG-7s.

The rich diet that I had enjoyed at the Z camps was not found at Luna Roja. We had rice and we had beans. That was it. For one month we ate rice and beans, with no fruit or meat to supplement the spartan fare.

Luna Roja was located on the side of a hill, and during the rainy season it was a heap of mud. Mud in camp was as much as eighteen inches deep in places.

Five hundred meters down the hill was a stream, our only source of water. One did not get up in the middle of the night for a drink because a five-hundred-meter trip down the side of a mud-covered hill had to be followed with a five-hundred-meter climb back up the hill. It almost didn't make sense to bathe, because by the time you got back up to the top of the hill you were just about as dirty as when you went down, due to slipping and sliding on the steep slope.

One of America's greatest contributions to Third World countries has been our public-health techniques. What we think of as common sense is often unheard of in less developed countries. As an example, when I first felt the call of nature at my new home, I asked where the latrine was. I followed the directions and found that it was on the same side of the hill and above the camp!

Morale was poor at Luna Roja. There had been several recent changes in command and the camp seemed to be divided into two groups: Pastora loyalists of the FRS and forces more democratically oriented and loyal to Alfonso Robelo's MDN. The camp was commanded by a Robelo supporter, Antonio, who was a chemist in civilian life and readily admitted that he had no military training or experience. Since he was favored by neither Pastora nor the supply officer at San Pedro, he was often back at headquarters begging and scrounging materials to keep the camp operating. We averaged two desertions a week during the fall of 1983. There were even thefts—almost unheard of in the Contra forces.

The second-in-command, our executive officer, a stocky Nicaraguan with an Abraham Lincoln beard, named Surdo, was a loyal FRS man. Surdo was often in charge because of the camp commander's absences.

At Luna Roja my primary duties included training both recruits and reservists. Pastora's guerrilla army had its own militia units. This was partly due to his group's logistical inability to maintain a large armed force, and partly because many of the refugees that made up the democratic forces also had families to feed. So we actually had "weekend warriors" who came up for a few days or weeks training, and then went back to the farms, subject to recall.

My training system was basic, practical, and real. There was neither time nor supplies to get fancy. But training at Luna Roja did include individual military skills and the small-unit tactics so necessary to jungle warfare. Unfortunately our training couldn't include marksmanship because we were so near the large Sandinista camp at La Noca. And La Noca's forces actively patrolled their area of responsibility.

I had to modify my training techniques, since Latins are not used to American procedures. Parris Island and Fort Bragg are in another world from these people. I would aim a kick at a Contra's ass because it stuck too high in the air during low-crawl exercises, and the other soldiers would be incapacitated with laughter. Even the man being disciplined would laugh! I tried to imagine a Marine Corps drill instructor's reaction to his men laughing when he chewed out a goof-off or kicked some recruit's butt.

Nonetheless, these Nicaraguan patriots trained hard, were enthusiastic, and never manifested any resentment at being ordered around by a gringo. They valued their training, knew they needed it, and knew that I was giving them the benefit of my own training and experience from the U.S. Army. It saddened me that many of them misunderstood my reasons for being there. As at the camps farther east, the men of Luna Roja continually asked if I was on active duty with the U.S. Army and if there were more like me coming.

But morale, political division, and vain hopes were less immediate problems. Dietary deficiencies, the rain, mud, and general lack of personal hygiene kept a quarter of the men out of action. At any given moment one man in four would be lying in his hammock, racked by chills and fever and plagued by vomiting and diarrhea.

"Antonio, a twenty-five percent sick rate is unacceptable. We've got to do something," I told the camp commander.

"Yes, Dr. John, but what can we do? We have so few rations. I give the men vitamins but still they get sick." Nicaraguans have an almost magical belief in the efficacy of vitamins. He shrugged and added, "Sickness is part of living and fighting in the jungle."

Carlos, the other platoon leader, and I had been talking with one of the neighboring farmers who had told us of a plantain and yucca field near the Sandinista camp. Yucca is a tuber used in place of the potato in most Central and South American countries. Combined with the tasty, potassium-rich plantain, our fighters' nutritional deficit could be partly corrected and the variety would improve morale.

An improved diet was vital to continue our operations. Besides, the field was in Sandinista territory. Our troops would gain tactical experience on the foraging patrols, and taking food from the enemy would raise their self-esteem. It certainly needed a boost. Antonio and I decided to incorporate these forays into the training cycle. Every class would harvest yucca and plantain as a graduation exercise.

Twenty-four of us set out, carrying our FALs, AD-47s, Chinese RPD light machine guns, grenades, and empty rucksacks. We marched through the dense jungle and crossed the border into hostile Nicaragua. This was war as it had been ten thousand years ago. It was as if my tribe

was raiding the gardens of another tribe. We
might kill or be killed for a bag of roots.

But if war is anything, it's primitive. And eating is both primitive and necessary. Therefore we
went into Nicaragua prepared to kill other men
for their food because we needed it to ensure our
own survival.

I was in charge of security for the patrol. After
we reached the field I set up the security squad in
a perimeter covering the two trails leading into
the cultivated clearing. The other men cut stalks
of the bananalike fruit and dug the yucca from
the ground. When our bags would hold no more
we withdrew as quietly as we had come, lugging
our booty back to Luna Roja.

Adolfo, a city boy from Managua, dogtrotted
ahead of me on the trail. A few months before he
had been a teller at a branch of the Bank of
America across a narrow street from Tomas
Borge's dreaded Ministry of the Interior. When
we stopped for a break to let our pounding hearts
slow down, he giggled.

"Que es chiste, companero?" I asked him.

"I would like to see the looks on the *piricuacos'*
faces when they come for the *platanos.*"

I joined him in subdued laughter.

Our luck had definitely taken a turn for the
better: When we reached Luna Roja the sounds
of our muted celebration drew a curious troop of
kongos in the trees over our heads. I sighted
through my FAL's scope at one of the monkeys.

"No, Dr. John. *Mucho sonido con el FAL.*" Antonio threw a .30-caliber carbine to me. *"Mata el mono con eso. Tu es un franco tirador."*

"En la cabeza, John," several of the troops shouted.

Sure, I was a trained sniper, but I had not been trained to shoot monkeys through their heads a hundred feet above me while they cavorted in the thick branches of jungle trees. Six shots later, two dead *kongos* were on their way to the cooks.

"Ha. *El franco tirador."* My *companeros* slapped me on the back. "What a sniper."

I didn't know if they were giving me a razzing for missing with four shots, for hitting one of the *kongos* in the ass instead of his head, or if they were sincerely congratulating me.

What difference did it make? That night we feasted on grilled monkey meat, boiled yucca, fried plantains, and—oh yes—rice and beans.

With some real nourishment finally under our belts, a training cycle completed, and our reservists arriving for the weekend, the men were hot for action. We got it . . . as usual, sooner than we thought.

Maybe they had discovered our incursion into their private garden patch and wanted revenge. Maybe they just wanted to ruin our sleep. Maybe the contact was an accident . . . one of their patrols might have gotten lost and wandered across the border into our lines. I'll never know.

I was lying in the dark in my hammock, rifle across my thighs, enjoying the unfamiliar pressure of a full stomach, having no idea that the Sandinistas were creeping across the border. A little before ten o'clock the familiar sound of the AK-47 woke me.

We were being hit.

My half gainer out of the hammock threw me in the mud on top of my rifle. I rolled to my left to pull the FAL from under me. It was unfireable, caked with mud. In my training classes I had demanded that soldiers be able to fieldstrip and reassemble their weapons blindfolded in less than five minutes. That night I met my own standards as I hurriedly stripped and cleaned the FAL in darkness so thick you could almost feel its blackness, like wet fur. Then I wriggled through the mud to look for the enemy. Gunfire crackled from fifty meters within the jungle, too far to see muzzle flashes in dense cover. I pushed myself up into a crouch and dashed from cover to cover, hip-firing as I ran to join the sentries.

By the time I reached the security perimeter the brush was eerily quiet. Tense whispers echoed in the dark when silence flooded into our little piece of the jungle. Our outposts had succeeded in driving off what was probably only a probe by the EPS, but we didn't sleep much the rest of the night, anticipating another attack. They knew where we lived.

We radioed San Pedro with the news that we had been probed and received orders to send out ambush patrols to intercept any more incursions from the Sandinista camp situated directly north of us. We were to depart two days later, commanded by Surdo, and launch an attack against La Noca. I was to be second-in-command of the mission as well as leader of the first ambush patrol.

We set up an L-shaped ambush just across the border on one of the more heavily traveled paths. The Sandinistas would be walking uphill across a clearing almost a hundred meters wide and half that distance in length if they came our way. With such a large killing zone, we should be able to take out a squad, I reasoned. I put half a dozen riflemen in a line just inside the jungle along the edge of the clearing closest to the trail. In the short leg of the L went an M-60 and two Type-56 Chinese light machine guns. I figured that such massed firepower would probably blow away anyone on the trail, while the riflemen would kill any flankers or survivors that tried to escape into the jungle. If any of the enemy tried to hightail it back down the trail or across the clearing to the jungle on the opposite side, they'd have a long run and little chance of making it to safety in the bush.

We waited in position from early morning through the steamy heat of the day—interspersed by several rain showers—until late afternoon, when an advancing *piricuaco* cautiously poked his head around a turn in the trail below us. Ever so slowly the eight Sandinistas came up the trail, duck walking in the peculiar manner of all Cuban-trained troops. Americans *walk* a patrol, perhaps in a crouch, but basically upright, with the weapon always swinging to point in the same direction the eyes are looking. But the Communists crouch into practically a duck walk and pivot their entire bodies from side to side, their AKs locked into firing position. It looks uncomfortable, and anyone who can ambulate like that for the miles the Sandinista patrol must have covered that day must have quadriceps made of steel.

I lined my telescopic sight up on the point man when he was fully in view, probably no more than eighty or ninety meters away from our well-camouflaged ambush. My pulse began to hammer as they advanced closer and closer. Every iota of energy was concentrated in taking up the slack with my trigger finger, controlling my breathing, and waiting . . . waiting for the last man to enter the killing zone . . . or my target to pass an anthill no more than twenty meters in front of me. He reached the mound of earth and I swallowed the last shallow breath I'd taken and gently squeezed the FAL's trigger.

BOOM! The impact of the recoil was lost in the cacophony of our massed fire as we annihilated the enemy patrol in one sustained volley. The Sandinistas went down as if their legs had been taken out from under them. It was over . . . so quickly. . . .

We rushed into the clearing, quickly gathered the weapons and ammunition of the dead and dying, administered the coup de grace to two mortally wounded enemy, and returned to Luna Roja.

My men were blooded. Now it was time for us to go on the offensive.

CHAPTER THIRTEEN

THE JUNGLE IS MEAN

With our reservists we numbered over sixty men fit for combat duty. We loaded up our two 60-mm mortars, five cases of mortar rounds, and one RPG-7 with seven rockets. We had two M-60s and an old Browning .30-caliber machine gun, known affectionately as *"La Treintra."* One man in each platoon carried a Chinese-manufactured Type-56 light machine gun. All platoon and squad leaders carried the robust FAL while the grunts packed the ubiquitous AK-47.

We set out through the rain forest at five o'clock in the morning, moving as Nicaraguans always move, quickly and silently. The silence of dark before dawn was broken only by the chatter of birds that heard us pass. In the distance we could hear *kongo* troops snarling and howling through their dawn patrols.

Nicaraguans are tough people. They live in a

tough country and they work hard to scratch out whatever living they can. They can carry heavy weights long distances, and no self-respecting *guerrillero* would think of going on a mission with less than five hundred rounds of ammunition in his pack.

Being an officer, I certainly couldn't behave any differently and I set out laden with four M-26 hand grenades, my FAL rifle, five hundred rounds of 7.62-mm NATO ball ammo, including ten full magazines. Three cans of tuna, three cans of condensed milk, extra socks, and medical supplies were in my rucksack. My pistol belt was loaded with my Colt .45 automatic, a Marine Corps combat knife, the grenades, and one of the few canteens at the camp. As an afterthought I slung a LAW rocket launcher over my shoulder in case we ran into a bunker. I was humping a lot of weight, but no more than anyone else in the column.

Nicaragua is not a flat country. Nicaragua goes straight up and straight down. The skyline is filled with extinct volcanoes covered with jungle. We walked on game trails and crossed streams that were bridged by logs sometimes no more than a foot in diameter. We went up and over mountains and down steep grades into the valleys between them. We forded a river, up to our necks in tepid, muddy water, with rifles held high over our heads.

Fatigue begins setting in after about two hours of such marching. On missions of more than one day our loads, including weapons, ammo, rations, grenades, and other gear, would be close to a hundred pounds. Carrying that much weight on level ground for several hours is quite a feat in itself, but in the jungled *montana* of Nicaragua, it borders on superhuman.

The pain begins in the upper back, right between the shoulder blades. You can tell when a *companero* starts feeling that pain because he'll begin tugging at the adjustment straps on the shoulder harness of his rucksack, raising the load higher on his shoulders. That always helps . . . for a while. Then the pain spreads to the lower back and sides—right under the floating ribs. The response to this new assault on the pain sensors is to lean forward and take some of the strain off the lower back. If you're going uphill at the time, your nose is almost touching the ground. It's too painful to be funny. By this time your breath is probably coming harder and harder, and your senses are starting to dull as effort focuses your attention on humping the heavy load, step by step. Rifles usually start sagging lower and lower. But you can't channel all your energy and attention into carrying this immense but necessary weight.

By now you are in enemy territory. Death can be waiting for you behind any tree. Around the next bend in the trail might be an illiterate Nicaraguan peasant, forcibly conscripted into the Sandinista Army, hiding in ambush with a Soviet-made AK-47 loaded with Warsaw Pact 7.62 × 39-mm bullets . . . with your name written all over them.

Your attention has to be first and foremost on that trail in front of you and the jungle on every side. Your eyes scan the ground for trip wires or the metal projections of an antipersonnel mine, the trees for snipers or trail-watchers, and the jungle itself for the snout of a machine gun or a glimpse of an uncamouflaged face or other body part. Whatever psychic energy and physical energy is left must be spent in directing rebellious muscles to endure even more pain and in planting your feet firmly. At times, when climbing the steep slopes, fighting mud and thick jungle foliage, you have to position your hand on your leg, just above the knee, and press down to straighten the joint, manually assisting your legs in taking the next step. In the deadly jungles of Central America you do not reach out for a vine or a branch to pull yourself up with because there's a fifty-fifty chance that vine or branch is covered with thorns or some other unpleasant phenomenon that ensures its survival and threatens yours. After hours of this kind of marching I've looked ahead, up the trail, where yet another mountain presented itself, and almost cried in anticipation of the pain awaiting me.

The brief glow of relief you might feel upon reaching the summit of these green grades is quickly dispelled by the difficulty of descending the slope without falling or sliding into the man in front of you. And you have to fight back only one scream of agony as your palm is impaled by inch-long thorns to learn that you never, never grab a branch or vine to slow yourself down.

All of this is difficult at best when you're heading out on a mission. But it's part of a low-budget war with only lukewarm support from the great democracies, and if you can't handle it, you shouldn't be there in the first place. The pain and exertion are multiplied considerably, however, when it's a return trip and *piricuacos* are on your asses like angry hornets. Maybe you're helping to carry a wounded man who will probably die in another half hour if you don't reach your lines, where there just might be a bag of plasma or at least some D-5-W to get into his veins. Sometimes on these headlong retreats your body screams at you more loudly than the wounded and dying. That's when, just for a brief instant, you think about saying "Fuck it!" and sitting down for a rest, taking your chances with the pursuers. But you don't. You somehow summon the strength and resolve to keep on going, step by step, until you can finally stop and rest your aching body in relative safety.

We rested twice on this eight-hour march through the green hell and finally neared the outposts protecting the Sandinista camp.

But the column halted and turned around. Then we probed another spot in the jungle. Once again the column halted and turned around. As the men filed back along the track I slipped to Surdo's side.

"What's wrong?"

"The dogs have posted sentries. They haven't seen us yet, though, and we're trying to find another path," the Contra leader whispered hurriedly.

I stopped him with a touch on his shoulder. "If we keep thrashing about, they're going to see us. We need to follow our plan. We need to infiltrate here."

"How? If the guard sees us, he'll shoot. Then the *piricuacos* will attack us."

"He can't alert anyone if we kill him," I pointed out.

"But the Sandinistas will hear our guns."

"Not if we cut the motherfucker's throat," I hissed.

Surdo's confused look told me that he either had no idea how to kill a man with any weapon other than a gun, or he had never heard that particular Anglo-Saxon sobriquet before. Since this obviously wasn't the time or the place to teach silent sentry removal, we moved off quickly to catch up to our column. For want of formal military training, the force had no choice but to attack the secondary objective.

Over sixty men had walked eight hours carrying heavy and valuable equipment through inhospitable jungle to be turned back by outposts manned by a handful of Sandinistas. That was the coarsest, simplest amateurism, out of place, I fumed, in such an important war. I plodded wearily along the trail, goaded by my anger and frustration. I composed a sarcastic speech suggesting that in the future we sent out recon patrols to establish the presence and exact locations of such outposts and that lessons be given in silent killing. Fury numbed my legs as we retraced our steps.

We returned to a hut we had passed on our way to the primary objective, set up our own perimeter defense, and settled down to a night's rest. Officers slept in the hut after the bats were chased out. After a day of exertion and frustration, a floor had never felt so good.

Before collapsing into a much-needed sleep I called my platoon machine gunner, El Gato Negro, and asked him to awaken me at three in the morning. Gato Negro, the Black Cat, was so named because he was the best we had when it came to silent movement and in the night he was seen only when he wanted to be. I told him that he and I were going on a special and secret mission and I was going to provide him with a valuable lesson.

There's really no excuse for the mission I planned. I would have been court-martialed in the U.S. Army, but I guess I was just plain pissed when Surdo scrubbed an entire mission because of a couple of lightly manned outposts. I needed to soothe my wounded pride. After all, I had been a recon trooper in the 82nd Airborne Division, trained in silent movement and killing, and was not used to having a well-armed force turned back by a handful of the enemy.

It seemed like I had barely closed my eyes when I felt Gato Negro's hand on my shoulder. Immediately alert, I rose from the floor and buckled on my pistol belt and load-bearing harness.

We slipped out of the hut, past our own perimeter guards, disappeared into the blackness of the thick jungle foliage and crept toward the Sandinista outposts. We crawled across a log spanning a small jungle stream and waded up to our waists through the swamp in front of the outposts. Moving slowly and silently, with only the thin light of the moon filtering through the canopy to guide us, almost before I knew it we were on the outpost. I heard the muffled sound of a sentry clearing his throat.

"Take this," I whispered, pulling a grenade from my combat harness and handing it to Gato Negro. "If they capture me, throw it at me."

"Por que?"

"Don't let them take me alive. *Me entiendes?*"

"Si."

I slipped behind the sentry, silently sliding the combat knife from its sheath. I rose up behind the Sandinista soldier, reached out, and grabbed him by his hair, pulling him down and back. His head snapped back and his spine arched as I struck downward with the knife. I'd meant to stab deep into the neck and rip the blade forward, severing the carotid artery. The victim loses consciousness immediately and dies in seconds when it's done correctly. But the Sandinista's greasy hair slipped through my fingers and I missed. But as he jerked convulsively to escape I managed to drag the edge of the knife across the front of his neck, cutting the windpipe. He wasn't mortally wounded, but he gurgled and rolled his eyes up and simply seemed to surrender. I plunged the knife deep into his throat as I had originally intended, ripped it out, and gently lowered the now lifeless body to the ground.

I backed away from his post and felt the cool waters of the swamp swallow me. I reached Gato Negro's side, tapped the signal that we would now head back to the hootch. We had little trouble getting past our own sentries, and when we were back at the hut, sitting on the steps, I asked Gato Negro if he had observed how I had done it.

"Done what?" he asked. "I couldn't see a thing."

I don't know whether to laugh over the absurdity of the situation or cry for the poor bastard that had just died for nothing. I just closed my eyes and went to sleep.

The day dawned clear and sunny—a bad sign —I like the rain. I like fighting in the jungle during the rainy season. It masks your footfalls. If you slip or break a branch in the thick jungle, with a background of heavy rain the sound won't travel more than a few feet. It restricts visibility and reduces the enemy's ability to see you coming. The rain is the jungle fighter's friend.

Fortunately, as we neared our secondary objective, the rain fell . . . hard. I was glad.

Our secondary target was a Sandinista command post directly on the Rio San Juan. At this point the river is well into Nicaragua, while down at the Z camps it forms the border between Costa Rica and Nicaragua.

Surdo and I had worked out a double ambush plan. I was to take nine men and, using maximum concealment, proceed to a point directly across the river from the command post. We would wait for the arrival of the supply boat, ambush it, and lay heavy fire into the command post. The sound of this action would, we thought, elicit a response from the nearby camp commander, whom we expected to then send assistance to his men under fire.

When reinforcements arrived we would ambush them, too, but with our main force.

The main body of our patrol, twenty-four men, was on a hill overlooking the command post and had an excellent view of about two kilometers of the river down which the relief would have to come. Mortars, machine guns, and riflemen awaited them. The rest of our patrol was spread along our escape route, guarding us from unpleasant Sandinista surprises on the way back to Luna Roja.

My men and I had to proceed down a hill that was thick with grass but in a direct line of sight with the command-post target. We low-crawled and slid, trying to get our bodies under the grass as we inched our way down the wet slope, directly under the guns of the Sandinistas across the river.

More rain began to fall, but just before I felt the drops I had raised my head a few inches, looked across the river, and had seen a Sandinista soldier looking out the window of the command post with a Kalashnikov in his hands. At this point I thought we were all dead: We had been seen and the mortars and AKs would open up on us any second. However, he didn't see us. There's a lot to be said for jungle camouflage fatigues, especially when seen against a background of solid green. It really works!

We finally arrived at the river and took up our positions. I was in the center with my LAW, a sixteen-year-old boy with the RPG-7 was at my right, and next to him with his light machine gun was El Gato Negro. Two men with FALs guarded our left flank, while behind and slightly above us, under the porch of an abandoned farmhouse, was the remainder of our team, armed with AK-47s. We were in an extremely vulnerable position and cleared fields of fire as best we could by low-crawling out to the edge of the river and trimming the tall grass with our knives, one blade at a time.

We then settled back to await the arrival of the supply boat. According to information provided by our spies in the area, the boat would be there in less than two hours.

We lay in the jungle at the edge of the river and endured a heavy downpour for over two hours. It cleansed my soul, to say nothing of my uniform. While I lay there waiting I reflected on my journey from a plush South Florida office to the very heart of the war between freedom and tyranny. I remember the flight into El Salvador and my surprise at seeing the green beauty of that troubled country. I thought of my stay in a Sandinista jail and the sadness of the people on the streets of Managua.

Then I remembered that I had learned at least

two interesting things in Managua. One was where all the old U.S. Army .45-caliber pistols went when they were retired. Every member of the FSLN seemed to have one of our old service pistols stuck in his belt. The second was where all the hippies had gone. Old hippies apparently don't die either—hundreds of them are alive and well on the streets of Managua. American refugees from the sixties haunt the streets and bars of the New World's newest Communist capital. With hair down to their asses, dirty, smelly, wearing Che Guevara T-shirts and Ho Chi Minh sandals, they try to be more Marxist than the Sandinistas. The big event on their social calendar was the annual Fourth of July demonstration at the U.S. Embassy.

Lying in the grass in the rain across the river from a Sandinista command post, I remembered tha vacant-eyed women with pale, translucent skin. They worked for Representative So-and-So or some left-wing "human rights" organization. And they chatted knowingly of the Sandinista junta's commitment to raise the standard of living of the poor while they sipped cocktails in the lounge of the Hotel Inter-Continental two blocks from the slums of Managua.

And I remembered my flight into Costa Rica and the good feeling of being able to breath free air again. But a cloud then crept into my thinking as I recalled my disappointment with Commander Zero and my realization that once again a hero had been found to have feet of clay.

I remembered the media ballyhoo about the

"charismatic" leader who seized the Palacio Nacional in Managua and hastened the downfall of the Somoza regime. This Nicaraguan guerrilla commander was billed as a military genius, a master of unconventional tactics, and a lovable man of the people.

I then remembered that he was also a member of the Sandinista junta after the overthrow of Somoza, Vice Minister of Defense. My Italian friend had told me that many in Nicaraguan and Costa Rican anti-Communist circles thought that had Eden Pastora Gomez been appointed Minister of Defense instead of Vice Minister, he would still be living in Managua and not in the jungles. "Closet Castro" was a term his detractors used to describe him. But these detractors were also fighting and dying in the jungles of Nicaragua as they struggled to free their country from the Castro-supported Sandinista regime.

When I was a member of his staff I had been appalled at his ignorance of basic military tactics. His soldiers were not trained in reconnaissance techniques, flank security, first aid, weapons maintenance, or many other skills that American military men consider basic. I had thought Pastora might have forgotten part of his education, but when I talked to people who had known him before his involvement in this conflict, it became apparent that the man had no military training, nor could he have been expected to have any. He had worked as a lumberjack, a shark fisherman, and a fishing guide for American tourists on the Barro Colorado in northeastern Costa Rica.

These were not the sort of occupations that would make one a Latin American Clausewitz.

Pastora was charismatic, no doubt, to Nicaraguan peasants . . . and journalists. These were the two groups who seemed to be most infatuated with his oratory and personal style. Oratory was Pastora's strong suit. Daily he harangued the troops from his safe encampment many miles from any action. His speeches, like those of his hero Fidel Castro, usually lasted from two to four hours and said little in the way of substance.

In the Z camps, when Pastora came on the radio all activity ceased and the faithful gathered around the radio, like disciples at the feet of the Master, while he spoke of this "revolution of love" that we were allegedly fighting for. I, frankly, was not there carrying on a revolution of love, I was there to help rescue a nation from tyranny.

At Luna Roja and the other camps much farther removed physically from Pastora's headquarters, only the officers of the Frente Revolucionario Sandino listened to the daily broadcasts. The troops preferred to listen to the FDN broadcasts. There they learned of actions, and plenty of them, as their brothers on the northern front slugged it out with the Communists on a daily basis.

I thought again of the romance between Pastora and the media. I remembered the arrival of a Cable News Network reporter, Chuck DiCaro, U.S. Army Special Forces reservist and former Air Force Academy cadet, who showed up at Z-3 one day in a dugout canoe. I helped him up the steep bank and hustled his gear up to the camp. Then he noticed my blue eyes, stuck a microphone in my face, and said, "You look like an American."

"No, Senor," I replied. *"Soy un Salvadoreno."*

Chuck was there to interview Commander Zero, and Zero did not like anyone else to be interviewed except himself. Knowing this, I avoided any other contact with the CNN journalist, who seemed eager to learn the identity and mission of this blue-eyed "Salvadorean."

Meanwhile, back in Nicaragua . . . the hum of an outboard motor brought me back to here and now. The supply boat plowed through muddy water toward the Sandinista command post.

My pulse increased as I opened the LAW and peered through the pop-up sights. The supply boat drew closer and closer, and as the sound of the outboard grew louder so did the pounding of my heart. When the prow of the Sandinista boat entered our killing zone, I pressed down upon the trigger button of the American-made LAW and . . . nothing happened. I shoved the safety forward once again, and once again, nothing.

Fortunately, the Chinese-made RPG did not malfunction and, simultaneously with my oath of disgust, the rocket grenade struck the bow of the supply boat, hurling two of its three occupants into the water. A second rocket finished them and our small arms opened up, raking the boat and the command post. The figure who had appeared in the window went down with lead in his chest, and still the murderous fire poured down upon them.

The Sandinistas never got one round off.

By this time I had thrown the LAW into the Rio San Juan, picked up my FAL, and was firing three-round bursts into the command post. I shifted my attention to the boat, which was now drifting in the rapid current. Through the FAL's scope I saw the outboard-motor operator lying in the bottom of the boat, apparently dead. But when I shifted my vision to his head I saw his eyes open and dart back and forth.

I thought, *You son-of-a-bitch, your comrades are dead and you think you're going to play possum and float on out of here. No way!*

I fired another three-round burst and saw the splashes on the near side of the boat—too low. I corrected, fired another burst, and saw the splashes on the other side of the boat—too high. *But*, I thought, *I've got you now, you son-of-a-bitch*. Three rounds slammed into his chest with the next burst.

A Sandinista soldier ran from the command post, and on my right El Gato Negro jumped up in his best Sylvester Stallone imitation, hip-fired his light machine gun at the fleeing figure, and caught him in the back when he was halfway to the cover he sought. Gato Negro was shouting at the top of his lungs, *"Viva Pastora!"* Boom-boom-boom-boom-boom. *"Viva Nicaragua!"* Boom-boom-boom-boom.

Not to be outdone, I jumped up and fired a

burst into the command post from my FAL and shouted, *"Viva Presidente Reagan!"*

We then withdrew up the hill, singly, covered by our comrades, until my detail was back at the top of the hill with the main body. We settled down to await the arrival of the Sandinista relief force. Our thinking was that they would have heard small-arms fire and a couple of rocket grenades, thought that a handful of guerrillas were harassing an outpost, and that they would send out a moderate force to deal with us.

Our plan worked. Two boatloads, forty Sandinistas in each boat, came around the bend of the Rio San Juan. AK-47 barrels bristled from the sides of the boats, making them look like fat porcupines waddling down the river. When I heard the sound of their motors I raised my head to get a look at the force coming to attack.

But the rain clouds had begun to clear and the river sparkled. Green billowed above green as ranks of volcanoes covered in every shade and texture of leaf crowded toward the horizon. Pointed peaks of jungle-clad cones crowned the edge of the visible world, and I froze in awed appreciation of the vista.

"Es hermoso, mi pais. Verdad?"

I turned to Pajarito, a veteran rifleman, and started to reply in the affirmative, but my breath was then taken away by the concussion of a mortar round leaving its tube behind me. An exhilarating symphony began as mortars, machine guns, grenades, rockets, and assault rifles played their deadly theme, repeated by echoes from the surrounding hills. The music was glorious. At times it almost burst the eardrums with a wall of pure sound. At other times each weapon's unique noise signature could be distinguished, as rifle and rocket played point and counterpoint. It was Beethoven's Fifth Symphony, Tchaikovsky's 1812 Overture, and every martial theme that ever raced through the frenetic mind of Richard Wagner, and it was all synthesized and mechanized, played by instruments of death. Its effect on me was almost sublime. For the first time in my life I could understand Patton, Napoleon, and other war-lovers. For the moment, at least, there was no greater glory than what I was experiencing.

Below us the Sandinistas were dying.

Most of them were dead before they had a chance to disembark on the banks of the San Juan. A handful made it to the cover of the jungle and returned our fire. Oh, yes, the Sandinistas did fight back. They were Cuban-trained and many were hard-core Communists who believed in their revolution.

Fortunately, we had established fire superiority early on and their return fire dwindled rapidly. I heard bullets hitting the trees over my head with a knocking sound and hunched a little lower in my position. After a few minutes only one AK answered our bursts.

We must have sent five thousand rounds after this one poor son-of-a-bitch before we called it a day and headed back by our prearranged escape route, picking up our road guards as we hustled through the jungle. As we left you could still hear the lone AK banging away at our former positions.

"Salud, mi enemigo bravo. We'll meet again."

CHAPTER FOURTEEN

MORE R AND R

After our return to Luna Roja the veterans cleaned their weapons and checked equipment while the new men slapped each other on the back and recounted tales of bravery and marksmanship that increased with each telling, even without the presence of *cerveza*. At our staff debriefing I mentioned the efficacy of reconnaissance patrols and silent killing and it was agreed that these really should be a part of the training of the army of the democratic alliance.

Surdo, busy congratulating himself on a successful mission, downplayed the wasted day and misspent energy of our attempt to hit the primary target of La Noca.

Our reservists cleaned their weapons and gear and returned them to the noncommissioned officer in charge of supply, changed into civilian clothes, and went home to their families, filtering away on horseback and on foot through the Costa Rican countryside.

Ryan and Chempena were at Luna Roja when

we returned. They had driven one of the jeeps and brought replacement parts for our radio and a few cases of ammunition. I hitched a ride back to San José after securing permission for a few days leave.

It was strange to find myself a few hours later in the bustling capital city of Costa Rica. San José was filled with shoppers who smiled and chattered to each other. Children ran boisterously through the streets and I found myself flashing back to Luna Roja with its sickness, bad water, poor rations, and the constant presence of death.

It takes mental resiliency to shift from one environment to another, especially when they are both intense and extreme in their differences, without slipping a gear or two. I slipped five or six that night.

I wanted to grab these *Ticos* and shout into their brown, bland faces, "Don't you know there's a war going on? Don't you know or care that a few hundred kilometers to the north people are dying to help free your neighbors?" Instead, I found a phone booth and put in a call to my wife, whom I expected to be at our *finca*. No answer.

I went to one of the American bars in downtown San José where I had previously spent some time drinking and learning what I could about local politics from the American expatriate community. When I walked in the door a few heads turned. I was frozen by their gaze, feeling I should start a speech. A fraction of a second later nearly everyone in the bar had ceased their chatter.

A hollow-cheeked forty-ish blonde with blue eyelids and scarlet cheeks stopped in mid-cackle, still showing her back teeth, though the corners of her mouth had already relaxed and begun to frown. Her older escort turned to follow her gaze, his glare turning to puzzlement as his eyes found me in the door. The bartender, a slick-haired *Tico* with a blue-black mustache and square-edged muscles barely poking through the loose fat on his thick bare arms, had seen worse, but I could tell he was wondering if he should move closer to the pistol he kept behind the bar as he absently polished a glass.

Patrons began quietly to return to their drinks, my urge to commit oratory passed, and I half stumbled into the dark interior, coming to rest against the cushioned bar the way a billiard ball with the right English nestles under the rail. I'd forgotten I was still wearing a uniform until I looked into the mirror behind the barkeep as he asked me what I'd have.

"Imperial," I told him.

While he rooted through the cooler for my *cerveza*, I stared vacantly across the bar, through the bottles, at the mirror. The cold bottle appeared in front of my clenched knuckles on the plastic-topped bar. He picked up the hundred *colones* I'd put on the bar and sprinkled my change in front of me. I didn't see him come or go. I was still watching the stranger in the glass.

Tiger-striped green and black faded into the

dark around him. Dark red hair bristled from the shadow under the brim of a bush hat. Only eyes lit the gloom. Whites showed all the way around the pupil, and they didn't blink. Their lines of vision didn't converge inside the building. Maybe they met a thousand yards away. Maybe they didn't meet at all. They were like the eyes in photos of grunts huddled beneath low stone walls in Hue, or the eyes that stare back from Matthew Brady photos from Devil's Den.

"What was it like up there?" the bartender asked.

I reached into the pocket of my field jacket, pulled out a hand grenade, and thrust my left index finger into the ring on the pin.

"How would you like to find out?" I asked. "Just keep the fuckin' beer comin' and leave me the fuck alone." I was in no mood for such a question. I told myself that I hated civilians and pacifist wimps who wanted to hear war stories but who wouldn't dream of putting on a uniform and carrying a rifle and a ruck to help out their neighbors.

Someone put a coin in the jukebox, and no one looked at me the rest of the time I was there. I sat in the bar polishing off *cervezas* one after the other. Periodically I called Alex and got no answer.

I began to fume, "Where the fuck is she, what is she doing, who is she doing it with, and what kind of shit is this when a man comes home for R and R and his wife's out running around?" About the time I was beginning to work myself into a

full-blown alcoholic paranoid state, the fellow I
rented the *finca* from came into the bar.

"Have you been up to see your wife?" he
asked.

"What do you mean been up to see her?"

"Didn't you know she's in the hospital?"

Rather than spending much time feeling like
the fool I was, I rushed out the door and took a
cab to the Clinica Catolica, where Alexandra had
been admitted, suffering from malaria.

When I walked into the hospital the sisters
took one look at the muddy boots and green uniform and directed me to my wife's room. She had
told them that her husband was a *combatiente*
with the anti-Sandinista forces and they had assured her that henceforth I would be mentioned
in their daily prayers. After the Sandinistas had
insulted Pope John Paul II during his Central
American tour, the gang in Managua were anath-
ema to good Catholics.

When I walked into her room she was awaken-
ing from fevered sleep. I closed the door and
walked to the side of the bed. Alexandra looked
at me, and without any expression of surprise, as
if I'd always been there, she asked, "John, why
don't you come back?"

I hunkered on the tile floor to keep from soil-
ing her sheets. Taking her dry, hot hand, I gently
whispered that I had come back.

Alex looked up, startled, and tried to raise her
head, but quickly sank back against the thin hospital pillow. "I thought you were a dream." Her
voice was thin and distant.

"No, I'm really here. I would've come sooner, but I didn't know where you were." I averted my face somewhat to keep from anesthetizing her with my breath.

She smiled a little and held my hand to her cheek. She seemed to doze for a minute. When her eyes opened again they looked less glassy. "What was it like?" she asked. "And what have you been drinking?"

"Alex, eighteen hours ago I was cutting a motherfucker's throat with this knife." I unsheathed the bloodstained Marine Corps K-Bar to show her. "Ten hours ago I was blowing people away and directing mortar fire on Sandinistas. Look at my face; look at my fucking face and you'll know what it's like.

"We've been kicking their butts, Alex," I told her. "It's not hide-and-seek, with us playing the rabbit role, like it was when I was with Pastora. And it's not like the U.S. Army, where you need permission just to put a magazine in your weapon, much less actually kill an enemy. I've seen more combat in the last few days than I ever dreamed of before.

"Alex, I have found it . . . I've found what I've been looking for in life. I have never felt so alive as when I'm walking those jungle trails with a weapon in my hands and every nerve tingling and every sense operating at full alert. Every step is important, every move you make may have life-and-death significance . . . my life, maybe."

"John, you don't like killing people, do you?" Alex had a puzzled look on her face and probably would have recoiled from me if she'd had the strength.

"No, no, I honestly don't, Alex. But I love this life and I love this cause—freedom. And I love the Nicaraguan people. They're so open and honest and kind. They're tougher than any group of people I've ever known, but they're also caring and gentle. And they want to be free so badly they can taste it; they want to be able to build a responsible nation that will guarantee freedom for their people. Alex, I've seen *campesinos* who could barely read poring over books on political science and American history, word by word, painfully teaching themselves these things they need to know to keep their country free once we win this war. One night I saw a Contra reading a translation of the *Federalist Papers* with a flashlight underneath a blanket. I really want to help them win, Alex, and soldiering is how I can best help.

"Soldiering is what I love—the camp life and the camaraderie with honest men. Fuck the wimpy civilians who smile at your face and stab you in the back for an advantage or a promotion. No, honey, I don't like killing. But this is worth killing for . . . and worth dying for.

"Yes, I have killed people, Alexandra. I've lain in the jungle, hiding in ambush for hours until the enemy came walking down the trail. I've lined up my sights on the center of a man's chest and tracked him while he walked into our killing zone. Then I've blown his heart out. The power is awesome, Alex, the power of life and death and the power you feel in knowing that, in a few seconds, this poor bastard is going to die—and he doesn't know it—and you're going to be the one to kill him. I've wondered what the guy might be thinking; maybe his feet hurt or he just got a promotion . . . who knows what's on those fuckers' minds? But you know that all of that cerebral activity is going to come to an end just as soon as you tighten your right index finger on that trigger.

"It's awesome, but it's not enjoyable. But I respect this power, Alex. It's like Grand Master Song taught us in *Tae Kwon Do* training, remember? 'The more power you have to destroy life, the more you will respect life,' he told us. And he was right.

"And it's not just taking lives, Alex, I've saved a few too. I've crawled on my belly to reach wounded men and start an IV or shoot them up with morphine and anticoagulants. I helped carry a boy half a day through the jungle, keeping a pressure bandage on him the whole time and praying that he wouldn't bleed to death.

"I love it, Alex. Even the jungle, although I curse it with an ever-increasing vocabulary when I'm sweating in it and humping a pack up and down the *montanas*. I love living in it and being able to live in it. I'm in there with people who are more primitive than you can imagine. Some of them had never seen a white man until I came along. And I'm right there with them, eating roots and lizards and armadillos and sometimes worse, but I'm not just surviving, I'm *thriving* on it.

"Look at me. I've actually gained weight and lost an inch off my waistline."

She was looking at me, and with a glow that I attributed to the fever. But then I noticed that she was squirming in the bed. We were both inflamed with passion over my proximity to the power of life and death and we made love right then in her hospital bed.

The next day I visited a safe house where fighters without families stayed when they were able to get a leave. The first man I saw was my friend Santiago. We embraced, grins splitting both our faces.

"Good to see you, John," he said. "I knew your luck was good."

"*Amigo mio*, it's good to see you. *Hombre*, I killed a *piricuaco* at three hundred meters with my FAL."

"One *piri?*" he inquired. "That's very nice. I killed thirteen near El Castillo last week."

I should have known better than to try to impress Santiago.

"Thirteen Sandinistas?"

"Yes, I caught them all at the river. The fools were brushing their teeth and washing, with no security out. The motherfuckers bought the farm."

Santiago had picked up some uniquely American expressions during his stay in Florida.

"Well, good for you, *companero. Y Aquila?
Como esta mi otro amigo?*"

"Aquila bought the farm, too, John. He was
walking point a few days after the big fight at El
Castillo and led us into an ambush. They blew his
chest apart with a machine-gun burst."

"Ah shit! Anyone else?"

"Bolivar got it in the same fight. Pedro, too."

I wondered if the motherfuckers couldn't kill
anyone but my friends. Bolivar, the lovable little
bullshit artist, would never brag about a piece of
ass again. And Pedro, a child of eighteen, would
never get that medical degree he'd talked about
when I'd met him at Tango.

Santiago and I went and got drunk. Roaring
drunk.

We cried and cursed and pounded our fists on
bars. We challenged *Ticos* and Americans and
anyone else who didn't like our noise to try to
shut us up. We would have piled their bodies up
and set them afire, offering the pyre as a flaming
memorial to Aquila, who just wanted choices in
his life; to Bolivar, who wanted to be free to be a
fuck-up; and to Pedro, who would have been a
doctor, serving the poor in his beloved Nicaragua.
Instead, three unmarked graves in the jungle provide the only memorial for these heroes' lives.

CHAPTER FIFTEEN

WAR CRIMES

A few days later, with Alexandra convalescing at our ranch, I returned to Luna Roja. I drove up with Ryan, Chempena, and several new recruits. On the way up Ryan told me to be prepared for some political changes. He told me that Commander Zero was unhappy with Robelo's pro-American sentiments and connections with the Central Intelligence Agency.

I told Ryan that my understanding was that Robelo ran the political section of the democratic alliance and Pastora's responsibility was strictly military. I had gotten this from Robelo himself. My fellow officer told me that this was not entirely correct, that Pastora's FRS was indeed a political movement as well as military and that very soon I would see that this was so.

I paid little attention to what he said after that. Complexities of Nicaraguan politics didn't really interest me. I was there to fight communism and follow my own agenda, not take sides in struggles where degrees of one's commitment to a certain political philosophy were important matters.

I actually had heard Nicaraguans arguing about whether someone was a Marxist or a Marxist–Leninist. Such subtleties of distinction were beyond my expertise. My doctorate was in psychology, not political science.

But I did file this hint away for future reference.

When I returned to Luna Roja I found the men eager for more action. I wanted to give it to them. The deaths of Aguila and Bolivar bore down heavily upon me and I wanted revenge.

After our attack on the command post and ambush of the would-be rescuers, motorized river traffic stopped for a while. Then, a week or so after my return, the Sandinistas got brave again and we could hear the hum of their outboards as they ferried supplies up to their outposts and down the Rio San Juan.

And once again our camp commander was back in San José begging for supplies. We still had not received canteens or shoulder straps for the packs. On marches I had seen men make bottles out of bananas leaves so that they could carry water with them. Most of the men ate their meals of rice and beans with their fingers and used plantain leaves for dishes. We were still extremely short on personal gear and weapons-cleaning equipment.

With Antonio away from the camp, Surdo was in charge once again and he announced a mission. Immediately after my return I had taken my platoon out on a few recon patrols and we had engaged the enemy in several short, bloody firefights. They were getting good, and we respected each other. I looked forward to the opportunity to lead them in another major engagement and was glad to hear Surdo's announcement.

Surdo planned the entire mission himself and told me that the planning was based on an order from Commander Zero. The basis for this order was Pastora's declaration that the Rio San Juan was henceforth to be known as a *zona de guerra*, a war zone, and that no traffic would be permitted on the river.

That made sense to me. The enemy was using the river to resupply and we shouldn't permit it. So it certainly made sense to deprive them of river transport.

But there was a catch.

The catch—as I learned in formation as we prepared to embark on this mission—was that there was also civilian traffic on the Rio San Juan. In fact, there was daily launch service between San Carlos on Lake Nicaragua and El Castillo, which had been retaken by the Sandinistas. I'll never forget Surdo's words as he gave his imitation of a Pastora harangue prior to our going into battle and he told the entire formation, *"Si mata una mujer, mata una piricuaca; si mata un nino, mata un piricuaco."*

In effect, Surdo was saying, "If you kill a woman, you're killing a Sandinista; if you kill a child, you're killing a Sandinista."

Off we went to kill women and children.

Once again I was to lead ten men who would actually perform the ambush. We followed our usual route into Nicaragua by the animal trails that slash in apparently random patterns across the jungle, but which always follow the path of least resistance. We set up road guards along our return route, peeling them off from the main body of the patrol as we proceeded to our ambush site.

This site, selected by Surdo, had only soft cover. There were no thick trees or rocks, only palmetto and vines. We cleared our fields of fire and settled back to await the arrival of women and children and whatever other civilian passengers there might be on this launch. Each man was alone with his thoughts. Not a word was spoken among any of us regarding the nature of this mission. Surdo paced back and forth nervously some yards behind us in the protection of the jungle. We waited.

The civilian launch was preceded by a Sandinista river-patrol boat with a .30-caliber Browning mounted on it. It roared by. The machine gunners inserted their ear plugs, and we all hunkered down a little deeper, locked and loaded, and waited. The loud throb of the seventy-foot launch's powerful diesels preceded its arrival by a good two minutes. The signal to commence firing was given just as the boat appeared in front of us, and, to my surprise and delight, I watched the RPG-7 arc over the boat and into the jungle on the opposite bank, where it exploded. The M-60 opened up. I rattled off a twenty-round burst from my FAL. Brass was flying as thick as the jungle insects as our entire squad emptied their magazines. Every bullet sailed harmlessly over the civilian craft.

When Surdo realized what was happening he came running out of the jungle cursing violently and firing his AK. I laughed aloud in relief and pride as we packed up and prepared to move out. Nicaraguan *compesinos* could be mean bastards and the toughest of soldiers, but they are not murderers.

My laughter stopped when I heard once again the now-familiar sound of an AK-47. This time it was incoming. Our ambush had been ambushed. One of the road guards had been walking a post as if he were at the front gate of Camp Lejeune rather than in enemy territory. He had been spotted.

The Sandinista counterambush arrived just after the civilian launch had passed unharmed and we were preparing to withdraw. There we were, no hard cover, exposed, with empty magazines in our weapons and under attack by a very angry enemy. They didn't know we had fired over the civilian boat and the Sandinistas probably felt very self-righteous and bent on revenge when they hit us.

This was, I guess, the only time in my military career that I thought I was going to die. The usual "God, get me out of this and I'll never do it again" ran through my mind. But then I asked myself what it was I'd never do again and calmed right down as the humor of the moment sank in. Of course the truth was that I wouldn't do anything differently . . . and if I died in the jungle, at least I would have died doing exactly what I wanted to do in this world. But I wasn't going to die if I could help it.

I tried to crawl under the earth as bullets clipped the surrounding jungle foliage. We rapidly reloaded and started returning fire, but targets of opportunity were hard to see because of the thick vines between us and the enemy. They knew where we were. And we knew where some of them were, but we didn't know how many there were or how many more might be coming in response to the sounds of the firefight.

I caught a glimpse of a mustard-colored Cuban uniform through the jungle and sighted through the scope. As I was taking up the slack on the trigger I recognized Alberto, a man who had just transferred into my platoon from Camp Indio Gigante. I recognized him just in time. We were so poor, our soldiers wore what was available. Sometimes all that we had in supply were captured enemy uniforms.

I burrowed deeper and fumed silently. I had almost killed one of my own men. We were on a bullshit mission—a mission that violated international law and all ideas of right and wrong. And we were led by a fool. Another fool had drawn attention to our positions. We were under fire from two sides. I was scared, pissed off, wet, tired, and—all of a sudden—sick.

In the middle of a firefight, with an angry enemy determined to kill us and, for all I knew, closing in, I came down with malaria. The fever burned until I thought the raindrops would turn to steam when they hit my head.

Then the Sandinistas broke contact. I don't know why. Things like that happen in combat, especially in the jungle, where it's often difficult to accurately assess situations. One minute we were cranking out rounds for all we were worth, shooting at vague puffs of smoke, half seen through the jungle . . . then silence.

We moved out, collecting our road guards on the way back. I alternately cursed and shivered as the disease tightened its grip.

We skirted an ambush on our route back to the border. The Sandinistas had a machine-gun ambush waiting for us, but on the wrong trail. They were on one running parallel to the path we were running on. They never saw us, but they heard our footfalls and opened up, raking the jungle between their ambush and our retreating band of *guerrilleros.*

I had put Gato Negro on road guard because I thought too highly of him to bring him on a mission to kill civilians. He was insulted. He might have thought that I lacked confidence in him. No way! He was an admirable man—about thirty, tall, lean, with sharp, handsome features. He had been a *campesino,* farming a plot wrested from the very edge of the jungle, when the call went out from Pastora. Like our pioneer American forebears, he had put aside his farming implements, picked up a gun, and answered the call to duty.

I motioned to Gato Negro and two riflemen to follow me. We moved off the trail into the forbidding green wall and returned the Sandinista fire as the rest of the patrol continued its headlong dash back to Costa Rica. The combined fire from the light machine gun and three assault rifles suppressed the Communist fire. We quickly disengaged and hurried after our *companeros*. As we pressed on toward the relative safety of Luna Roja, and I became weaker and more delirious, Gato Negro carried my pack and, finally, my combat harness. When I at last staggered into Costa Rica only my FAL and a fresh magazine weighed me down.

I reported to Surdo that I was seriously ill and that I was going to evacuate myself to the Contra hospital in San José. Furthermore, I told him, I intended to make a full report of this mission to San Pedro. Surdo snarled but said nothing as Gato Negro stepped forward, his right hand resting lightly on the handle of his ever-present machete.

With Gato Negro both guarding and helping me, we left Luna Roja. We borrowed two horses from collaborators at a nearby farm and began what turned out to be a two-day journey through rural northern Costa Rica.

Sometimes I knew where we were. Sometimes I didn't. Sometimes the trees marched by with supernatural, microscopic clarity, and at other times the foliage merged together in a great, mold-colored, liquid blur until I felt like a puffy white fish swimming on the ocean floor.

In my fever-induced delirium I talked to dead friends, old lovers, and people I'd read about but never met. My past was compressed into sporadic instants of thought while the painful moments stretched into infinity all around me, as nothing but memory seemed to move or remind me of who I was as I drifted in this private green hell. The verdant soul of the jungle soaked my eyes, my ears, my tongue, and my brain. In my sickness the beauty and terror of the jungle's omnipresent green haunted my lapses into consciousness.

If one has never been in true jungle, it's impossible to know how the color of vegetation moves into everything. First, of course, the leaves are green. Every visible surface, far and near, is the color of chlorophyll. Then moss covers much of what would otherwise be brown bark. And emerald-colored algae fill every rivulet down every trail. Every insect and every snake steals the color of the leaves. And filtered light tinges everything that struggles to have independent color.

Universal green was bad enough when I was well; it can produce feelings of claustrophia in sound, normal men. But with the malarial fever, the monochromatic universe had me near madness.

Villages passed my eyes like pictures at an exhibition. I can only remember brown people, thatched huts, the muddy trail, the pain . . . God, the rhythmic pain in my joints as the horse's protesting gait punctuated my dull misery. The trip took two days. Gato Negro carried me from my horse to a board bed padded by a rag mattress. It was in the rear of a *cantina* in one of the nameless villages that dot the edge of the jungle. The *dueno* charged us twenty *colones* for the accommodations. He was proud of having such a fine bed and mattress with which to host the sick *Senor* and threw in a blanket and pillow—a sack stuffed with more rags—gratis. I gratefully pulled the blanket up to protect my body from further ravages by the mosquitoes and let my head sink back onto the humble pillow.

I awoke somewhat refreshed but still quite miserable and dreading further punishment from the saddle that Gato Negro had thrown onto my horse. I gritted my teeth and mounted, cursing the pain.

We finally reached a passable road later that day. We were met by a jeep sent by the alliance to fetch me in response to a radioed message from Luna Roja. The driver stopped at a safe house in Ciudad Quesada, about halfway to San José, where I was examined and given chloroquine and aspirin by a Contra doctor. That evening I was back at the *finca* with Alex.

CHAPTER SIXTEEN

ENTER THE COMPANY

While I was recovering from this first bout with malaria, the growing rift between Robelo and Pastora was reported in the Costa Rican press. Pastora had accused Robelo of sending Democratic Alliance troops loyal to MDN into Honduras for training by American Special Forces. Robelo, in turn, revealed that Pastora had, through his adjutant, Carlos Coronel, made contact with Fidel Castro. Pastora had asked the Cuban dictator to pressure the FSLN into making a separate peace with FRS. The Contra commander used the Democratic Alliance military radio to make broadcasts in the clear, denouncing Robelo.

Each accused the other of multiple wrongdoings and Pastora threatened to shut down military operations unless Robelo resigned and gave him sole leadership of the Democratic Alliance. This was what I had been forewarned about: The accusations Pastora made against Robelo were pure fiction, what Harry Truman used to call a "red herring." The true motivator of this fratricidal bullshit was Pastora's desire for complete power on the southern front and his dream of being the maximum leader of post-Sandinista Nicaragua.

I made a report against Surdo for ordering us to kill women and children. I was told that he would probably be removed from his position as executive officer of Luna Roja and dishonorably discharged from Pastora's forces. As it was, nothing happened to Surdo. Instead, when I was well I was to be transferred to another zone of the war.

That's typical of armies. Problems are solved by removing the complainer rather than addressing the issue.

I was to serve under Dr. Hugo Spadafora. He had recently resigned his command with Pastora because of the Castro affair and had become military commander of the southern Miskito Indian forces of Brooklyn Rivera.

Spadafora, a medical doctor, was formerly the assistant director of public health in the Republic of Panama and had resigned to become a full-time fighter against the Communists in Nicaragua. I didn't mind serving under Hugo, but I was no longer happy in the service of Eden Pastora.

Fighting with old weapons against an army equipped with the latest in Soviet armament, I can handle—fighting with limited equipment is part of modern guerrilla warfare. But knowing that fifty kilometers down the river there was plenty of good gear that was not allocated to your camp because its commander was not a loyal follower of Pastora, *that* I had trouble dealing with. I didn't care for military operations commanded by fools whose only qualifications for command were their left-wing beliefs and personal loyalty to a megalomaniac.

I also resented our relatively limited number of actions when the FDN forces of Colonel Bermudez were fighting every day on the northern front. However, the FDN was led by conservative businessmen like Adolfo Calero and anti-Communist church leaders who were politically unpalatable to the leftist Pastora, and he would not join with them. While I was under his command he refused to coordinate attacks with FDN campaigns, attacks that might have taken some of the pressure off our allies and, perhaps, allowed their forces to seize a major city or a province and establish a provisional government.

Morale, perhaps needless to say, was very low throughout the Alliance.

Luna Roja had split into two camps after I left. One was commanded by Antonio and loyal to Robelo. The other half was commanded by Carlos, the FRS lieutenant. These groups didn't fight each other, but they did become two completely separate units.

During the split between MDN and FRS and the rest of the Democratic Alliance, several other things happened to undermine the situation. The most important was that MDN cut off logistical support for the troops. This led to wholesale desertions and the end of most combat operations.

During one week toward the end of November or beginning of December 1983, six hundred combatants left the line. Some of these took their weapons with them and sold them for food in Costa Rican border towns. AK-47s could be bought in Los Chiles for as little as five hundred *colones*—about thirteen dollars in American money at that time. One group from Luna Roja hijacked a bus north of Ciudad Quesada and got free rides back into the interior of Costa Rica. The rest of the troops were hungry, as stored supplies started to dwindle. Many military and political officers left the democratic alliance, some giving up their part in the struggle, disgusted. They began looking for civilian jobs with which to support their families.

Some of these formed other groups and vowed to carry on the fight against the Sandinistas independent of Robelo or Pastora. One of these was the *Movimiento Tercero*—the Third Movement—known more simply as M3. It was headed politically by Alvaro Taboada, who held a doctorate in political science and had been the Nicaraguan ambassador to Ecuador at one time. Its military commander was my old friend El Gringo. I was steered into an affiliation with M3 by an unexpected "coincidence."

While convalescing from the attack of malaria I went out very late one night to stretch my legs and enjoy a meal at an out-of-the-way restaurant in a San José shopping center called El Pueblo. It's one of the few places in San José where you cannot only get a decent steak but you can get it at almost any hour of the day or night. This particular night I was in there at about 3 A.M. While waiting for my meal two men joined me in the nearly deserted restaurant. One was Raoul, a Costa Rican I had met on a previous trip to the capital.

He had manifested considerable interest in who I was, what I was doing in Central America, and for whom I might be doing it. The other fellow turned out to have been in my old outfit in the 82nd Airborne Division! I had barely known him then and hadn't seen him since those glory days of yesteryear.

They asked me how I was handling the split among the southern Contras. I replied that I was disillusioned, not only with the fratricidal split, but also with Pastora's military leadership, the horrible logistical situation, and the amateurism of some of Pastora's lieutenants.

Raoul then suggested that I investigate the group known as M3 and said that if I did so, and participated in some military operations with them—without pay if they couldn't afford to offer me any, he stressed—that I could very likely find myself being asked to do some other things for other groups and earn some very good paydays.

This sounded interesting, especially the part about future paydays. I had returned the stipend given me by the Democratic Alliance; their treasury needed it more than Alex and I, but it had been a while since I'd had any income. Money wasn't a problem just yet, but it soon would become a consideration. And I remembered that everyone in the business in San José considered Raoul to be a CIA contract agent. He was known to often do things on his own—free-lancing—and had even financed an operation or two with his own money.

He told me that if I went along with the program he'd described and did some things for M3 that I might be tapped to join the elite group of mercenaries based in Panama who had mined the Nicaraguan harbors and pulled off the Porto Corinto raid for the CIA. They had blown up most of the oil-storage facilities in the country by this time, I'd been told. The soldier-without-fortune label given me by one of my *companeros* was only too true. Maybe it was time to make some money for getting shot at.

I left Raoul and my former acquaintance and the next day got a call from El Gringo. He had heard from Raoul that I wanted to talk to him. I said that we definitely had mutual interests and that it might be a good idea for all concerned. He made an appointment for himself and Dr. Taboada to meet me at the Hotel Irazu that evening.

They were early—a sure sign that they needed me. Taboada explained that he had been invited to become a member of the executive council of the Frente Revolucionario Sandino. Various high-level Nicaraguan political leaders from the democratic left were asked to join this council and work out a political platform. They took the task very seriously and spent hours in meetings and negotiations to hammer out the FRS platform. Then, at the end of all their efforts, they were told that the truth of the matter was that they were going to be a rubber-stamp council. Pastora was the leader of FRS, but he wanted this council, which would second all of his pronouncements and policies as a token show of democracy.

Big egos were involved here, former ambassadors, monsignors, professors, and medical doctors. They were important men in the exile community and were highly insulted by Pastora's announcement.

Taboada, by the way, had come down from the diplomatic and academic ivory tower and had carried an FAL through the bush. He might have been in on the El Castillo raid. I know that he saw some patrol action around the time of the assault on that ancient citadel. He had not been afraid to put his ass on the line for democracy.

"Dr. John, you have suffered for our cause. It is not just to you or to us that you should be used and discarded this way. The democratic forces fighting for a free Nicaragua have a place for a man with such talent and dedication."

El Gringo was a calm, persuasive, reasonable man. His un-Latin disciplined restraint earned him the sobriquet "El Gringo." Nicaraguans thought he'd spent too long in the States and it had turned his brain American. His *norteamericano* ways, perfect command of stateside English, and his counterrevolutionary stand might have led some to believe that El Gringo was a lackey of U.S. interests.

Quite the contrary. El Gringo was a barely converted Communist. He had fought in 'Nam with the North Vietnamese Army, I had been told by unimpeachable sources. He had been trained in special warfare in Cuba. Terrorist tactics had been his course of study from Libyan instructors. El Gringo's beautiful Chilean wife had been an Allende supporter who had fled to Costa Rica, joined the FSLN, and fought against Somoza in the last war. They had met on the battlefield, fallen in love, and married. They had been the ideal revolutionary couple.

But El Gringo was a Nicaraguan and a patriot. He had not quite understood the worldwide ambition of Communist revolution. And when he acquired a reputation for outspoken criticism of the Sandinistas' Cuban masters, the Communists marked him for death. He and his wife fled to Costa Rica.

"American friends of mine have promised help for M3, Doctor. A squad of Cuban–American volunteers, all veterans, is on the way from Miami. M3 will have a military arm composed of two branches, one a battalion-sized regular army outfit to be trained by a smaller cadre. That cadre will, in turn, perform special operations.

"All of this cadre will be veterans, if not of the U.S. Army, at least of the guerrilla war against the Sandinistas. Are you interested?"

I took a long drink of my Cuba Libre. "I would like very much to be included in your plans."

Smiles and toasts went around the table.

It sounded like a good plot. I could make some

good money, doing good work with good men. And since the soldier-without-fortune venture with the Democratic Alliance hadn't worked out, maybe a little hard-core mercenariness was appropriate. And if this was a Central Intelligence Agency operation, maybe the company I'd be in would be more professional.

I told El Gringo and Taboada to count me in. But I needed to see my wife first. They agreed to await my return.

Alex, weakened by the recurrences of malaria, had left for the States. And the stress of her work in the clinic and her fear for me hadn't helped.

I returned to the United States and passed through Washington, D.C., where I contacted an old friend. When he learned what I had been up to he mentioned that some friends of his on the Hill might want to talk to me. That sounded fine, but I was in a hurry to see Alex. I went on to New York to visit with my wife, but the very next day I was contacted by a man who identified himself as a staff member of the House Intelligence Committee. He requested that I return to Washington immediately.

The dome of the Capitol looked more imposing than ever to me as I walked up the steps. I had been in this building before as a tourist and as an invited witness before Representative Donn Edward's subcommittee considering legislation on the missing-children problem. That had been in my days as a psychologist, but now I was going in by invitation of a little heavier committee, and certainly in a different role. I gave the guard at the entrance the extension I had been told to ask for.

"But this is a restricted number," the guard snapped.

"Dial it," I countered.

A few minutes later a man in a rumpled business suit came out, shook my hand, and escorted me through the rotunda into a drawing room where he pulled aside a curtain that had concealed a door. We went through it, down a narrow hall, and into a large, elaborately furnished conference room.

I was debriefed for four and one half hours by persons without names. Some were lean and hard and had the look of intelligence and special operations about them. Others were younger and softer-appearing. They all took notes. Questions were incisive and demanded exact answers.

First they had me describe Pastora, Robelo, and the other Contra leaders physically. I guess this was to ascertain that I really did know these people. Then they had me point out the various camps I'd been to and the locations of some of the larger engagements on detailed maps of southern Nicaragua. They demanded detailed accounts of the battles: numbers—ours and theirs —weaponry used on both sides, tactics, and apparent strategies.

They asked me if I'd ever witnessed direct participation by CIA agents. It was phrased thusly: "Have you seen, with your own eyes, any participation by the Christians?"

CIA case officers called themselves "Christians

in Action"; free-lancers knew them by another name. "No," I responded, "I haven't seen any of the 'Clowns in Action' in any combat operations." Several jaws around the table clenched at my flippant answer. "Sorry 'bout that," I murmured.

A pale, youngish-looking man seemed to sneer when he asked if I'd come across any Cuban troops in combat. He looked satisfied when I also answered that in the negative.

"But," I quickly went on, "I did see Cuban soldiers in Managua and, shortly before I arrived at Z-3, Pastora's people captured some East German medics on the Rio San Juan. They were released to the Costa Rican Cruz Roja. This was documented in all the Costa Rican newspapers," I added.

I continued, relating reports from the Democratic Alliance's intelligence sources inside Nicaragua that the presence of terrorists from the Palestine Liberation Organization and Irish Republican Army, as well as Cuban and Libyan troops, had been confirmed many times. I told them about the ammunition boxes with Arabic lettering that Aguila, Santiago, and I had found. My young questioner squirmed and stated abruptly that he had no further questions.

After this marathon session I was told that there were others on the Hill who wished to speak to me and I was escorted into the Rayburn Office Building and met by more nameless men whose questions were even more precise. And my photos of Nicaragua that had disappeared into the mys-

terious colonel's pocket reappeared in enlarge-
ment, drawn from stiff, pale manila folders. It
was nearly midnight when I left Washington and
headed across the Key Bridge into the Virginia
suburbs.

My friend and I went deer hunting the next
day in the Virginia mountains near Front Royal.
While waiting in the blind he mentioned that
there were some other people in the area who
wished to talk to me about doing the same thing
for them that I had been doing for the Contras.
He went on to tell me that we just happened to
be near the house of one of the fellows who
wished to talk to me. I agreed to stop by and
listen to what they had to say, but only after I'd
gotten the deer I'd come for.

The driveway had several "No Trespassing"
signs down its length and I noticed large dogs
patrolling the grounds. A Mercedes with diplomatic license plates was parked near the house, as
were several other expensive cars with ordinary
Virginia tags. We were met by a tall, lean, light-
complexioned black man whom I noticed wore a
large pistol under his coat, and wore it well.

A professional, I thought.

This fellow escorted us inside and served tea
and small cakes while we waited for the man who
had requested my presence. After a few minutes
he emerged from a back room and I heard a car
start. I noticed that the car with the diplomatic
tags was pulling out of the driveway.

This was my first meeting with Eduardo. A
young man, pale but stocky and athletic, he had

been, he told me, the chief of security for the Surinamese Embassy in Washington, D.C., before that country's takeover by Desi Bouterse, a Marxist.

"We are unknown to most of the world, and our country is tiny. But that is no measure of our love for freedom. We want to regain our country and we want you to help us."

Eduardo was forward but precise. I didn't mind being approached directly, and I had been thinking about getting out of the Central American quagmire. And I was beginning to need money; we'd been living off my savings and the proceeds from the Mexico operation for nearly a year.

"I am empowered," Eduardo continued, "to pay you for your time. We want you to prepare a plan and tell us what you need to rescue Surinam from the dictator Bouterse."

I agreed to consider his proposal. Eduardo supplied me with several maps of the country and a brochure describing Bouterse's takeover and the establishment of a Marxist dictatorship in Surinam. I noted that the book had been produced by a group called the Council for the Liberation of Surinam. He also showed us a video-taped history of the coup d'état and several resulting purges. He also claimed that the tape had been produced for the council by the Central Intelligence Agency. It was a slick and professional piece of work, dramatic yet informative. It could have come from Langley.

I agreed to study the situation and perform my

own investigation into what he had told me. But I declined to discuss money until I had completed my investigation. We parted with a handshake.

My newfound undercover fame filled most of my thoughts for the rest of my time in Washington and my return to Costa Rica. I returned to San José and learned from Dr. Taboada that relations with the Democratic Alliance were very bad. Pastora and Robelo, at least temporarily, had patched up their feud and FRS had rejoined the coalition. I was told that Pastora was very angry at the people who had left the Alliance, including me, and planned to make an example of M3's disloyalty in particular.

Long before I'd left the Alliance, disillusioned, I had called the number given me by the Pentagon colonel and had been in fairly constant contact with a representative of the American government throughout my stay in Central America. It was time to contact him to pass on what I had been told and ask for advice on my next move. He suggested that I "continue with M3 but keep your back to the wall while in San José." I passed on Taboada's request for American assistance.

He looked at me for a second, smiled, and said, "Every Nicaraguan in San José has his hand out. When M3 does some significant damage to the Sandinista economy, *then* we'll talk about aid."

That seemed fair enough to me.

I reported this conversation to El Gringo and suggested to him that we try to pull something off. He thought this was worth further consideration and took me to a meeting at a safe house in

San José. There I met a Nicaraguan who had served with the American Special Forces in Vietnam, several other Contras who were dissatisfied with the coalition, and a Colonel "Alvaro" of the FDN.

Alvaro was Central Casting's answer to a call for a Latin military officer: tall, muscular, with a shaven head and a constant scowl. He was perfect for the role. He was also a graduate of the U.S. Army's Command and General Staff School at Fort Leavenworth, Kansas, and had been a lieutenant colonel in the Guardia Nacional of General Anastasio Somoza.

We discussed plans for FDN to supply M3 with small arms, mortars, and plastic explosives. We also drew up plans to attack a power station near the town of San Carlos in southern Nicaragua. Surely this would get the CIA's attention and provide funding for this new outfit. However, M3 was too poor to even purchase the explosives necessary to pull off the mission and promised supplies from FDN hadn't materialized. They never did.

El Gringo came up with a scheme to raise the money, since the M3 political wing had been completely unsuccessful in their fund-raising efforts. He would lead a group of M3 *guerrilleros* into Nicaragua, where they would steal cattle from a state-run cooperative farm, herd them back into Costa Rica, and sell them to ranchers along the border.

I thought long and hard about this. And eventually I had to tell El Gringo that I had come to

Central America to fight communism in solidarity with my Latin American neighbors. I had not come to Central America to be a cattle rustler. Even though I saw the need for the operation, I could not, as an American citizen, engage in this type of activity. He replied that I should stay in San José and provide security for the political officers.

He and five other M3 *guerrilleros* left early one morning for the border. At noon that day, while I was guarding the M3 offices, a call came in saying that we would never see El Gringo or the other fellows again. They had been kidnapped.

Our agents in Ciudad Quesada reported that they had recognized some of Pastora's men pulling over the M3 vehicle with drawn guns and abducting El Gringo and the others. By six o'clock that evening we had confirmed all reports.

The day before El Gringo and Taboada had played a tape for me. They claimed it was the recorded intercept of a radio broadcast from San Pedro to Pastora in the field. San Pedro had been reporting the location, size, and probable armament of the M3 camp. I recognized the voice of Commander Zero saying in Spanish, "Maybe we'll just go down there [to the M3 camp] and start another war."

At that point I had had enough.

My enthusiasm and idealism had been blunted by the harsh realities of politics within the Contra organizations. My initial reason for coming to Central America had been to ascertain which side was the "right" one, become part of the war, and ingratiate myself to those with whom I was fighting so that I could build a new life and career south of the border.

I had certainly discovered the right and wrong sides of the Nicaraguan civil war: The Sandinistas were bullies and thugs with no respect for civilized conduct, much less human rights. And the Contras, for the most part, were very decent men who had literally pledged their lives, fortunes, and sacred honor in their attempt to establish freedom and democracy in their country. But there was Pastora—at best a pathologically narcissistic megalomaniac whose desire for ego gratification and power for its own sake detracted from the noble purposes of the rest of the Contra leadership. At worst, as had been strongly suggested by a NATO intelligence source, he might even be a KGB operative who was deliberately sabotaging the anti-Sandinista coalition.

Whatever the reason for the internal strife, I had no desire to be part of it. I had made up my mind to accept death on the battlefield; I had even prepared my wife and family to accept the possibility that this might happen. The cause of freedom was worth dying for, but a knife in the back or a grenade blast while I sat in a *cantina,* because I had thrown in with the wrong faction, was not what I had bargained for in Central America.

Besides, the Surinamese had offered money—decent money—as well as an equally good cause and an equally despicable enemy.

I telephoned the embassy duty officer and briefly told him what I had to say. Five minutes later the phone rang and my American contact listened to my full explanation of the day's events. After thanking me for the information he told me, "Get out of Dodge."

He didn't need to tell me. I was already gone.

CHAPTER SEVENTEEN

FINALLY, A PAYCHECK

I returned to the States and left a message at Eduardo's contact number saying that I had begun work on the plan he had requested and, unless I heard otherwise from him, I would consider myself on the Council's payroll at the rate of two thousand dollars a month for the planning stage. This would increase to five thousand dollars a month during combat or in-country operations. I received a call later the same night. A heavily accented voice said, "Okay," then the receiver clicked. I was working on my first mercenary venture.

Besides preparing an operational plan of attack on the Surinamese capital of Paramaribo, I had studied the political material that Eduardo had given me at our first meeting. The material had described the coup in which Bouterse and a handful of other sergeants had taken over the entire country, the purges and murders that followed, and the makeup of the resistance group known as the Council for the Liberation of Surinam. It was led by Dr. Henck Chin-A-Sen, a former Prime Minister and President of Surinam. The Council was directed by a committee headed by Chin-A-Sen and several industrialists, labor leaders, and representatives of the media.

In early January 1984 I met with two council members, Mohammed and Glen, at Eduardo's heavily guarded house in Washington's suburbs. I presented my plan.

It called for an all-out assault by air and land on the capital city. Price tag: a million dollars.

Eduardo had told me to count on recruiting 150 mercenaries. The Council would provide 250 Surinamese freedom fighters. At this first meeting, however, the equation changed. The Council could come up with only a dozen or so dependable Surinamese, whom, they said, should be used primarily as guides and interpreters.

In my original thinking I had planned to recruit M3's fighters, make a cash donation of so much per man to the organization, and return the Nicaraguans to Costa Rica in possession of all military equipment and armament used in the Surinam operation. I had tentatively discussed this idea with El Gringo and the M3 leadership and it had been approved in principle. After this first meeting with Council members I again contacted M3, told them of my increased personnel needs, and was told that they could provide between three hundred and four hundred men.

Glen and Mohammed were still in the country and received my message that I would be able to provide the entire assault force. They took this plan to the Council in Holland and called me a few days later. The Council liked the plan, but they wanted documentation of the existence of my mercenary army and the transport necessary to get them to Surinam.

Men were no problem. And I was sure I could find aircraft. Central America is full of old DC-3s, some of which are completely unairworthy, but bargains can be had. Every other Central American, it seems, is a pilot and I anticipated no difficulties in recruiting one who could fly straight and keep his mouth shut. I told Glen that I would have to make a trip to Central America and at their expense. I would return with verification of the men, their training camp, the availability of transport, and the war matériel we needed.

Glen hesitated and then told me that there was a possibility that the Council would be unable to raise a million dollars. Could I make optional plans with a lower price?

The original plan really was rock bottom. It provided for a well-armed force sufficient to capture Paramaribo and neutralize opposition but with little slack. Cheaper operations could not win the country immediately but would possibly unite opposition to the Bouterse regime within the country and lead to a long-range victory.

I developed two more plans, one of which called for a hundred-man invasion of Nickerie, the western coastal province of Surinam, and a protracted guerrilla war. The other plan called for a platoon-sized force of Nicaraguans, American Vietnam veteran mercenaries, and a half dozen Surinamese who had Belgian Army Commando training. With this platoon I planned to take Nieuw Nickerie, the provincial capital, inflict maximum damage, and count on the Council to use resultant publicity to solicit contributions. Then we'd finance a real coup d'état. If no help came, I would extract my men either by sea or across the Corantijn River, which forms the border with Guyana.

Glen was delighted with these plans and went back to the Council. He phoned later and told me that my trip to Central America was necessary and that the expense would be borne by Chin-A-Sen himself. I departed the next morning for Costa Rica.

Taboada and El Gringo, recently freed by Pastora, met me at the airport. I handed them an envelope stuffed with American hundred-dollar bills and told them that this was a token payment to show them good faith of the Council. Since M3's fund-raisers had been batting zero, the money was gratefully received. El Gringo had a list of equipment that he considered necessary for the operation. He and I went over his list, crossing out some of the luxury items such as starlight scopes and extra boots for every man. I didn't blame El Gringo for trying to get everything he could for his men and his movement, but I knew the Surinamese wanted a bare-bones budget.

While waiting around San José for a ride up to the training camp where I planned to take pictures to furnish the Council, I stopped at the Nashville South, an American bar owned by two

American veterans. A fellow slid up next to me
and said that he and I needed to talk. Since San
José is known as a city of gays, I thought the guy
had made some kind of mistake.

But when he said that he understood that I
needed an airplane, the hairs on the back of my
neck stood up.

Could this really be happening?

He then told me my real name and a good bit
more about myself, what I was doing, and for
whom I was doing it. He went on to state that he
could help with all of my needs. We retired to the
back room of the bar at that point to ensure pri-
vacy and told Jack Phillips, one of the owners, to
see to it that we weren't disturbed. He nodded in
the affirmative and brought us fresh drinks before
I started talking to this stranger.

He told me his code name was "The Hippie"
and he said that there were people in Costa Rica
and the United States who wanted to see my
present mission succeed and that he would intro-
duce me to others who would not only furnish
aircraft but long-range radio equipment as well.
The Hippie asked me for a list of arms that would
be needed and I furnished him with the list that
El Gringo and I had worked out. He told me that
we would meet again that night at my hotel.

That evening I stopped by the Key Largo.
When I entered, the owner, a former U.S. Army
Counter Intelligence Corps officer, whose acquaintance I had made shortly after my arrival in
the country, was holding court at his favorite table in the corner. Jimmy was regaling a crowd of

Costa Rican whores and American journalists with a tale of my encounter with three thieves at a beach town on Costa Rica's Pacific coast. He whooped when he saw me and rose from his seat, dislodging the cute *Tica* that had been perched on his lap. "Well, look who's here," he cried. "Bruce Lee, himself."

Jimmy had been present at one of my R and R excursions. I had caught the three thieves coming out of my hotel room with my diving gear in their hands. Jimmy and Jack Phillips had helped me and the police load their unconscious bodies into the Costa Rican equivalent of a paddy wagon. Every time he told the story it was expanded, until this night he had me battling twenty-five thieves single-handedly and laying them out.

Ignoring the crowd at his table, Jimmy walked over and clamped me in a vise-like grip.

"There's someone I'd like you to meet," he told me, and guided me toward a willowy blonde seated at the bar.

"Angie, this is Dr. John. You two have a lot in common," he said to me. "Angie has a Ph.D. and she's an ex-Marine just like you, turkey."

The blonde captured my attention completely. I never even saw Jimmy leave us and return to his boisterous table. Angie was tall and slender, with the grace of a dancer. While not the prettiest girl in San José, she had a face that piqued my interest—full, sensuous lips—and a dancer's body that aroused another sort of interest.

"So you were a BAM?"

"That's right," she countered easily, ignoring

the bawdy implication of those initials. "A Beautiful American Marine."

We returned to the lounge at the Irazu in time for my scheduled meeting with the Hippie. Angie waited in a corner booth while we talked.

"Everything on your list will be provided," he told me. "You realize that these things can't be bought here in Costa Rica."

"What do you mean?" I queried.

"Evidently," he told me, "most of your list is going to be filled entirely gratis. The M-16s, machine guns, mortars, and ammunition are going to be given to you for this operation. Tomorrow morning, meet me at six o'clock in front of the Nashville Bar. I'll have more information for you. Don't be late."

Jesus H. Christ! Who are these guys and why are they taking such good care of me? I wondered. I returned to Angie, deep in thought as the import of the Hippie's message slowly sank in.

We went on that night to other bars. I was captivated by her grace and easy banter. We ended up at my hotel room, quite drunk and clutching each other in frenzied lust before the door had closed behind us.

The next morning when I awoke Angie had gone. She had left a polite and appropriate note. I cleared the fog from my brain with ice water and aspirin and opened my briefcase. Sure enough, the little Scotch Tape indicators I had learned to place from reading a James Bond book told me that its contents had been examined while I slept.

Angie was either a thief . . . or a spy.

I took a cab from my hotel to the Nashville Bar and pulled up at exactly six o'clock. The Hippie was sitting there in a farm truck waiting for me.

"Glad to see you're on time, Dr. John," he told me. "Sorry to get you down here so early, but I have a lot to do today."

"I'm an early riser," I lied. "What's up?"

"You'll meet me here again tomorrow morning, same time," he told me. "Be ready to travel. What time's your flight out?"

"I leave on LACSA's noon flight to Miami," I told him. "I have to be in Brussels Tuesday to meet with the Council."

"That's cutting it close, but we can fly you back from the ranch to the airport. No problem."

"That's it?" I asked.

"No," he answered. "I want you to check me out with your embassy contact."

He scribbled his real name on a scrap of paper and handed it to me.

"This is no bullshit, John," he told me, fixing me with a hawkish stare. "You're a lucky man to be leading a sanctioned operation so early in your career."

I left the Hippie and breakfasted on *gallo pinto* and *huevos fritos* at a nearby Nicaraguan-style restaurant. I sat and sipped a *cafecito*, waiting for the embassy to open.

I called my contact's number and arranged for a meeting later that day. When I arrived my contact pumped me for a play-by-play description of the Washington Redskins' recent play-off victory over the San Francisco 49er's.

Interesting set of priorities, I mused. But having lived in the Washington area for over twelve years, I, too, was a Redskin fan, and I was soon reliving the game in vivid detail. He chuckled over the disputed pass interference call at the game's end that ensured a Super Bowl trip for the 'Skins.

I reported my contacts with the Council for the Liberation of Surinam and described the proposed operation against Bouterse. I was rewarded with a briefing on the terrain, meteorology, and racial makeup of the country by another fellow who had always sat quietly during my meetings with this contact. I had avoided mentioning any of what had transpired between the Hippie and me, but I did present the scrap of paper he had given me and asked my contact if I could talk to this fellow. He glanced briefly at the name, half smiled, and said, "Sure, go ahead. Why not?"

I left the office after a promise was extracted to bring some Super Bowl souvenirs on my next visit and was escorted to the door. When I opened the door, to my surprise, Angie was sitting on the bench waiting to come in next. She almost fainted when she saw me. Evidently they hadn't told her whether I was a good guy, a bad guy, or what, but only that she should monitor my activities and provide an inventory of what materials might be in my briefcase.

"Hello," I said. "Will I see you later?"

"Uh, sure," she stammered.

I returned to my room at the Hotel Irazu and slept the rest of the day. I had just risen, showered, and was dressing to go out to dinner that evening when I heard a knock at the door. I opened it. There stood Angie.

"Make love to me, John," she said.

I did.

The Hippie and I drove up the mountain road, leaving San José as the sun broke over the mountains.

"You know Angie works for the Company, don't you?"

"Huh-uh, ah" was all I could come out with.

"C'mon," the Hippie said. "A chick who's been in the Marines, with a Ph.D. in political science? Who the fuck did you think she worked for?"

"And you, Hippie? Who do you work for?"

The Hippie smiled and shifted into a lower gear as we started down a long grade. "The Company recruited me fresh out of Virginia Military Institute," he told me. "I've done three things for them in fifteen years. They've made me a rich and happy man. I own a pineapple plantation in Puerto Rico as well as the *finca* up here in Alajuela. This is the fourth time I've been asked to do anything. I was sitting in that fucking hillbilly bar in San José waiting for you for two days. Now I'm taking you to meet 'The Ranger' and he'll control you from here."

The Ranger was an impressive man, tall and thickly muscled. He was Latino but spoke English with a Midwestern accent. He showed me the DC-3 and invited me to photograph it and to verify to the Council that an aircraft did indeed exist.

"Now we can't get your whole platoon there in one DC-3, but don't worry. There will be another aircraft. You might as well use this ranch as your training camp and staging area," he said. "That way there will be less traffic in and out of here. We don't want to alert the *hijo puta* Costa Rican security people."

When I had taken sufficient pictures to guarantee to the Council that a camp existed and that aircraft were at our disposal, the Ranger walked me over to a Cessna 150 and told me that his son would fly me back to the Juan Santa Maria International Airport in San José to make my flight on Costa Rica's national airline, LACSA.

"All your Surinamese friends have to do is come up with the money for the uniforms and other soft gear, we'll handle the hardware and the commo equipment. Don't worry about weights, loading, and fuel requirements. When will you know about the Surinamese?"

"I'm supposed to leave tomorrow for Europe. From what I've been told, they should have the money to me within two days. I expect to be back here within a week to start moving the M3 people up."

"Good," he answered. "Take this number, and when you have the money call collect . . . for yourself. Then we'll know you're ready and start things happening down here. *Hasta luego*, Dr. John."

Thirty-six hours later I was at Luchthaven Airport in Brussels. A message from Mohammed awaited me at the Capitol Airlines counter. I went to the indicated hotel and waited. The next day, Glen, Mohammed, a Surinamese expatriate businessman introduced as "the Fat Man," and a Surinamese physician showed up. The plans were laid out for the Fat Man's inspection, as he was supposed to be the main financier of this operation. He told me that he had been ripped off for three hundred thousand dollars by a Belgian mercenary who was supposed to have trained Surinamese refugees and then lead them in an operation against Bouterse.

Later I learned the real story. The sum was not three hundred thousand dollars, but three hundred thousand Dutch guilders—about ninety thousand dollars. Also, the Belgian had trained a platoon of Surinamese and not just in basic military skills. He had put them through parachute training in addition to marksmanship and other individual skills.

The Surinamese left and advised me to stay close to the hotel in anticipation of their message. The next night I got a phone call. The Fat Man had decided he did not trust Americans and, therefore, he was not going to put up any money. Glen asked me to continue on my retainer for the Council, that they would try to raise the money for some kind of operation against Bouterse.

I returned to New York in a quandary. I had received no instructions on how to report failure to the Ranger. If I made the call, they would think the mission was going to proceed and start certain wheels turning.

At first I was angry at the Ranger and his people. Why the hell didn't they just furnish the whole works? Why the condition that the Surinamese put up a share of the financing?

When I thought about it, however, it made sense. After all, it was *their* country, and if they wouldn't show good faith by helping to finance the rescue of their homeland, how could we trust them to do anything else? Also, if the Ranger and the Hippie really represented the Central Intelligence Agency, as they and the embassy contact had led me to believe, then for them to completely finance the operation would be seen as a cynical America overthrowing a foreign power to install a puppet government, if it ever came out.

While waiting for further contact from the Council I returned to Washington to visit old friends. After about a week I received a call from Costa Rica.

It was Angie.

"How did you know where I was?" I asked.

"Never mind that," she snapped. "The Hippie is very upset that he hasn't heard from you."

"I was unsuccessful in Europe," I told her. "And I had no instructions on how to get him negative news."

"I'll tell him."

"Will I hear from you?"

The buzz of the dial tone as the circuit broke was my answer.

CHAPTER EIGHTEEN

ENTER THE PENTAGON

I needed help. My head was spinning from the events of the past few days—much less the past few months. Less than one year previously I had been sitting in my office on Oakland Park Bouelvard in suburban Fort Lauderdale wondering if I should fight a false, malicious accusation or chuck the whole thing. I was now living with my decision, but I needed guidance.

As a psychologist I'd turned to my former professors when confronted with a baffling case or equivocal responses to the Rorschach inkblots. Early on in private practice I'd learned that the academics were not only better sources of objective information, but a hell of a lot cheaper than the private practitioners. Once I had called a colleague with whom I also socialized and asked him a question about the significance of a spike on a Minnesota Multiphasic Personality Inventory profile and had received a bill for fifty dollars from him in the next day's mail for the "consultation." Being taken to lunch at a modest restaurant delighted the low-paid professors.

But I didn't know any Stateside intelligence types at all, much less any who would provide a consultation for a free lunch, and there was no listing in the Yellow Pages for the type of consultant I needed. I did, however, remember a Washington-based journalist I'd met in Central America. He'd asked questions that were a little more incisive than the average *periodista* and, to the best of my knowledge, some of the answers never appeared in print or on the evening news. Maybe those stories were filed at a different desk than that of his editor.

I called the journalist from a pay phone, gave him the number, and asked him to call me back from another pay phone. Five minutes later he was back on the line. I told him that I was in town and that I desperately needed to speak to someone in the intelligence community. I referred to it as "the business." I went on to tell him that my problem did not involve a Russian plot to kidnap William Casey or anything of earth-shaking import, but that some very weird things had been happening in my life recently and I needed some help in straightening them out. "Further," I told him, "some of these weird things are perishable and will probably be of interest to somebody upstairs."

I'd learned that words like *business, perishable,* and *upstairs* were buzz words in the intelligence world.

"I'll call a friend," the journalist told me, and hung up.

Less than an hour later the pay phone rang again. I ceased my pacing and lifted the receiver.

"I'm having a party Friday night," the journalist said. "You might want to stop by. I'm *sure* there'll be at least one person you'll enjoy meeting."

Someone's interest was piqued.

Damn! I thought. The only thing better than having connections is having Washington, D.C., connections.

I wondered what to wear. The safari suit was definitely out. For one thing, it was freezing; for another, I'd stand out like a sore thumb and that would violate what I had been told was Rule One for intelligence types. I selected a dark three-piece suit with a white shirt and a regimental striped tie. Buttons, not cuff links, I thought. Can't stand out in either direction. My red beard and ruddy complexion are enough to draw attention to me no matter how I'm dressed.

On a cold, sleeting night in February of 1984 I navigated a rented Lincoln Towncar up Wisconsin Avenue to the journalist's surprisingly posh Georgetown apartment. His live-in girlfriend, a six-foot redheaded dancer, greeted me with a kiss and ushered me in. She then announced to one and all, "Hey, everybody! The mercenary's here."

So much for my carefully planned junior-executive cover. I slunk into the party. It was, I suppose, a typical Washington after-work affair: hors d'oeuvres that signaled gastric distress contrasting with expensive wines and brandy. Further contrast was not apparent in the assembled guests, however. Snatches of conversation seemed to reveal a commonality of political conservatism that linked them all.

The journalist's position in the Washington pecking order was also revealed: There were Senate staff members present, but no senators; oak leaves glinted from the uniforms of the few military men, but no general's stars were to be seen. My host and benefactor was "in," but not at a very high level. So be it. He had the wherewithal and the friendly disposition to put this party together on short notice to cover my meeting with an intelligence officer, a meeting he had arranged. I put my snobbish thoughts to rest and mingled while waiting for a contact. I didn't know if a man in a trench coat was going to hiss at me from behind a potted palm or what, so I busied myself with a drink and small talk.

I drew a blank on the requested rum and Coke, settled for a brandy and soda, and fended off questions about who I was and what I did. I assured those who asked that the redhead was joking, that I had only been in Central America to research the refugee problems. The conversation was easily turned to the fascinating world of politics, in which they all lived and breathed.

The cute blonde was on the staff of the Vietnam Veterans of America. A young man who had gone heavier on the brandy than the hors d'oeuvres worked for a conservative Southern senator's committee; his friend, who steadied him when necessary, was on the same senator's staff. We were joined by a tiny man who, judging from his pithy conversation, was blessed, or cursed in the Washington environment, with a genius-level IQ; he was a senior staff member for Senator Jepsen of Iowa. Also in the group was a steely-eyed ex-Ranger who provided security for journalists on overseas assignments in high-risk areas. He said little but probably didn't miss a word that was said.

These people were real, and all were doing important jobs, but I kept glancing toward the door. I really couldn't get too interested in Capitol Hill gossip or political causes. Things that were more important to me were waiting to be resolved.

Partly from anxiety, I suppose, and partly from boredom, I decided to test my hypothesis that all of the journalist's guests were radical conservatives. "I wonder when Ted Kennedy will finally make his bid for the presidency?" I asked of no one in particular.

Icy stares were directed my way. "Just kidding, folks," I muttered, and went to freshen my drink.

My host signaled me to follow him to the den at the rear of the apartment. The man I'd come to meet had slipped in by the side door, the journalist told me.

I stepped through the door and into a dimly lit room. The walls were covered with military memorabilia from the journalist's assignments in many lands. An impressively filled bookcase took up one wall and leather furniture completed the impression of studious masculinity, which matched the journalist's public personality. Sitting in one of the easy chairs was the man I'd been waiting for.

I gaped in disbelief. The officer unfolding a six-foot-plus frame and extending his hand could have doubled for Chevy Chase—the actor/comedian, not the Washington suburb. I didn't know what to say. There I was, primped and primed for a clandestine meeting in the city that pulses with power, hoping to discuss matters that not only affected my life but that might mean freedom for a nation, and my contact looked like a comedian.

The deep voice that rumbled forth was not one to induce levity though. "Dr. John," he said, "I'm sorry to have kept you waiting, but Washington traffic goes crazy when a few flakes of snow fall."

The voice helped me shake off the feelings of panic that had arisen when I'd first seen him. "You're right about that, Colonel," I replied, after checking his shoulder boards and seeing the silver oak leaves. "I used to live in the area." I remembered the years of fighting the traffic on the Shirley Highway. The infamous "Mixing Bowl," which funnels traffic from the George Washington Parkway, Interstate 95, and the Pentagon parking lot onto the Fourteenth Street Bridge, had provided plenty of thrills, especially when there was precipitation.

Our host discreetly withdrew without a word,

closing the door behind him. We sat and silently appraised each other for a brief moment. I saw in front of me a tall, athletic, prematurely gray field-grade officer whose uniform boasted five rows of fruit salad with campaign ribbons and battle stars from Korea and Vietnam. His highest decoration was a Silver Star.

Medals for valor often mean a lot less on the chests of high-ranking officers than the same decorations on an enlisted man. Commanders in 'Nam, and I'm sure in other wars and other armies, used to write each other up for commendations and medals. Grunts and NCOs would risk death to save wounded buddies or accomplish missions, only to see their recommended decorations for valor downgraded because too many Bronze and Silver Stars had been passed out that month to field-grade officers whose bravest moments probably came when they didn't foul their trousers during VC rocket attacks on their HQ.

But the screaming eagle of the 101st Airborne Division adorned the right shoulder of this youthful-looking lieutenant colonel's uniform. That and the Combat Infantryman Badge and jump wings on his chest indicated that he had more than likely earned his Silver Star. No, this guy was no desk-bound administrator who had hopped into a chopper and flown into a hot area for a brief visit to beef up his 201 file. Whoever or whatever he might be, he was definitely for real.

I don't know what he was thinking as he sat there, apparently sizing me up. His gaze was benign but at the same time intense, as if he were memorizing every detail of my tanned and scarred face, yet wanted me to know that I was in friendly territory.

"Tell me how I can help you." His voice was almost soft, yet firm and clear, completely belying the baby face and other similarities to the famous comedian.

I began, slowly at first, then in a torrent of words, to narrate my odyssey from academia to the war in Central America and my present involvement with the Council for the Liberation of Surinam. "I seem to keep getting teasers from the Central Intelligence Agency," I told him after the initial rush of words. "First, there was the embassy contact given me by the bird colonel who had shown up at my jungle camp on the Rio San Juan." I named the man and his position at the U.S Embassy in San José. "This guy would pump me for all I was worth, then at other times he'd call me over to the embassy—all very hush-hush—and all he'd want to talk about would be the Washington Redskins or the weather.

"When I was with M3 he'd say things during our meetings like, 'When M3 pulls off a mission against an economic target in Nicaragua, then we'll talk about American aid.' He'd never make a direct statement or give me instructions. It was always a hint or a vague suggestion.

"The whole M3 thing was strange," I continued. "I was steered into the group by a Costa Rican who everybody in the business down there says is a contract agent for the Company." I related the scene in the restaurant when I'd been approached by Raoul. "And how's this for a coincidence?" I asked rhetorically. "He was accompanied by a pilot I'd served with years ago in the U.S. Army.

"Now there's this Surinam business, which really has me confused." I told him about the contact with Eduardo and the other Council members, Angie, the meeting with the Hippie and the Ranger and the deal we'd apparently worked out. "They never came out and said they were CIA, but who else would provide arms and equipment for an operation against a Marxist government? But," I said, thinking out loud, "would the CIA be so dumb that they'd forget to give me a code to report the failure of the Surinamese to come up with their share?"

The colonel laughed. "We'll get to that, John. But first things first. You've told me a lot and, as far as I can tell, you haven't told me one lie. So we're off to a good start.

"Let me tell you first that I'm from DIA—the Defense Intelligence Agency—and even though we're very interested in private and semiprivate military operations, we are forbidden by law from participating in any way. So if you're looking for sponsorship, I can't help you."

"Colonel, I just need some help in making sense out of what's been happening—if there's any sense to be made out of it. And maybe a little advice on how to handle the Surinam business."

"Okay," he replied, "that's basically what our friend told me." He gestured in the direction of the door. Through it we could hear muted laughter and the clink of ice cubes being dropped into a glass. "I wanted to make sure that we understood each other.

"You have told me the truth. But . . ." He paused to light a cigar he had extracted from an inside pocket. He puffed vigorously, until the tip glowed evenly and his head was wreathed in smoke. "You didn't tell me the whole truth. I'm not going to say that your life is exactly an open book, but I was able to obtain some information on you rather easily." He reached into a black briefcase at the side of his chair and extracted a yellow, lined notepad. The pages he flipped through were covered with thickly scrawled notes.

"Let's see," he murmured. "There was military school, Junior NROTC, U.S. Marine Corps, U.S. Army, reenlistment, an all-expenses-paid tour of Southeast Asia, then college on the GI Bill, a master's degree, Ph.D.——then, all of a sudden, you pop up on DEA's computer as a debt collector for a major cocaine dealer. Mind explaining that last item, Doctor?" He emphasized the last word with just the faintest trace of sarcasm.

I sighed and related the story of my discontent with the practice of clinical psychology, the false accusation, and the ensuing investigation and my disgust with the lack of support from my colleagues. I briefly related the origin of my interest in the world of Latin American politics and my desire to involve myself in that world.

"So the mission for the cocaine dealer was sort of a refresher course in paramilitary operations and a means to get enough money to support my wife and I while I searched for another career," I explained.

"Well," he replied, "there couldn't have been much more to it or the Drug Enforcement Agency would have done more than open a file on you." He paused to study his notes, puffing contentedly on the cigar. "Somebody else opened a file on you about that same time. What's this about a trip to Cuba?"

"Cuba?" I almost shouted. "I don't know anything about a trip to Cuba."

"My mistake." He smiled. "How about a visit to a Cuban Embassy? Know anything about that?"

They didn't come any smoother than this Pentagon colonel, not in my experience.

"Oh, that was on the mission to Mexico to recover the funds this dealer's lawyer had skipped with," I said. "We'd picked up a rumor that our target was negotiating with the DGI for sanctuary in Cuba in return for turning his contacts in the States over to them."

"Sounds like a Vesco deal," the colonel mused.

"Exactly," I responded. "So we went to the Cuban Embassy in Mexico City under the pretext of obtaining visas to visit their country. The Cuban government was sponsoring a deep-sea fishing tournament and they'd made a big play at attracting American fishermen. We thought we might be able to get some information on other Americans going into Cuba—where they might be staying, that sort of thing. In retrospect, our thinking was pretty naive. I had no idea that the Cuban intelligence service was one of the most highly rated in the world.

"Our conversation with the lady in the visa office must have been monitored, because the minute we started asking questions a European came into the room and whispered something to her. Two minutes later we were being hustled through the gates and told not to come back. It went from *'Bienvenidos'* to *"Adios, gringos'* just like that," I said, snapping my fingers.

The colonel chuckled and put the notepad back in his briefcase. He turned his attention to relighting his cigar and soon had it glowing anew.

"Continue," he said.

"Well, that's it as far as any contact with Cubans, except for the ones that are fighting with the Contras," I assured him. "And the ones I photographed in Managua."

"I'll continue then, since I'm reasonably certain that you're not running drugs through Central America or playing footsie with the DGI," he said, with the hint of a smile playing at the corners of his mouth.

"For one thing, I cannot and will not give you advice," he told me. "What I will do is give you the benefit of some of my experience with our friends out at Langley. But whatever decision you make is your business, and after tonight I don't know you, nor have I ever met you.

"I don't know if you've ever entertained any notion about working for them directly, as a contract agent." He paused, as if expecting a comment.

"Well," I admitted, "that was mentioned by Raoul, and frankly I did have some hopes of getting in on some of their operations."

"You can forget that," he said, not unkindly. "With your background you are probably considered a loose cannon that they don't want rolling around on their deck. You're too independent and have too many connections with what they consider the wrong kind of people. Not that they don't have an interest in you . . . or, more precisely, your activities. I'm sure they do, and especially after your run-in with the boys in Managua, they have probably monitored your movements in Central America and Europe, and maybe even here in the States."

"But what about Raoul and the Hippie and—"

The colonel raised a hand to silence me. "Let me finish," he admonished. "All the people you've mentioned, with one definite exception, were more than likely contract agents or free-lancers who get a bone from the Company once in a while. As you've no doubt learned by now, there are no monopolies in the intelligence business.

"With your contacts in the Contra movements and your bona fides well established down there, you could be a valuable commodity for a free-lancer trying to sell an operation to the U.S. government, or some other government for that matter.

"I have no doubt that your friend in the embassy is Company. In fact," he continued, "the position he holds is often a cover role for the CIA station chief of a country. His calling you over there to talk about the weather was very likely to demonstrate his control over you to someone above him. There's no doubt at all that you are on the inside of the Nicaraguan counterrevolution, and if one of Langley's agents has a degree of control over you, then you have some rating as an intelligence source. But a man who has run errands for drug dealers, including an armed operation inside a friendly country . . . well, there's just no way you're going on their payroll. I'll bet you were never signed into the embassy in San José, were you?"

I remembered that I had been steered around the sign-in log at the entrance on all my visits.

"Here is the way they probably see you, John. You're a man with talent. You can put an operation together from planning through execution and you can even liaison with the politicians. That makes you a dangerous man. If they can control you through the embassy and a few bones thrown to you from their contract agents, they'll do it. If an operation fails, they don't know you and there's no paper trail linking you to the United States. If an operation succeeds, don't expect anything more than what you can get from the foreign nationals involved, like the Surinamese Council, for instance.

"But know this, John. If you look like you're uncontrollable, from their point of view, they'll stomp you."

"You mean kill me."

"Possibly. Or you could find yourself pulling long, hard time in a foreign prison.

"But it's not all gloom. I believe that you are motivated by altruism, but you wouldn't mind making a nickel while you're at it. Am I right?" He winked.

"Colonel," I responded, "if I could spend my life fighting for freedom and make a decent living at it, I do believe I would be a happy man."

"Good luck, John," he said, rising from the chair. "Get as much of a commitment as you can from whoever you're dealing with in these operations. Be cynical. Try to get something on whoever you're dealing with and put it in a safe place before you let them know that you have them covered. Always be ready to bail out at a moment's notice. The will of the Company often translates to the whim of the Company. Remember what the referee says, 'Protect yourself at all times.'"

We parted with a firm handshake and a sincere "Thank you" on my part. I returned to New York to mull over what this DIA colonel had told me and to wait to hear from the Council . . . or somebody.

CHAPTER NINETEEN

SURINAM 101

It was half-past nine on a Saturday night, and my contract with the Council was going to run out at midnight. The phone rang.

It was Glen. He was in Miami, and asked me how soon I could get there. I took a cab to Newark airport and arrived in Miami about two o'clock Sunday morning. There I met with Glen and Roy, a tall, lean man with a café-au-lait complexion. Roy had been a first lieutenant in the Surinamese and Dutch armies. I later learned that he had been a Dutch intelligence officer for about twelve years.

The Dutch, according to my information, didn't want Bouterse overthrown. I had already been told by my embassy contact in San José that the Dutch Secret Service was actively protecting Bouterse. They may well have had a hand at putting him in—before they knew of Bouterse's deal with the Cubans—and they don't want the boat rocked any more, he told me. "The whole mess may end up being the Dutch version of Watergate," he had said.

Roy and Glen informed me that two dozen Surinamese, most with prior military service, were at a camp in French Guiana. They wanted to hire me to train them and ultimately lead them into battle in Surinam, according to my plan to assault Nickerie. At this point I had been advised by friends in Washington and some other veterans to drop these people. But I decided to take the job for the worst reason in the world—I needed the money.

So I agreed to continue my two-thousand-dollar monthly salary from the Council and go to French Guiana to train these people. If the Council could arm them and supply them, I would take them into battle, provided they hired one other American.

After a few debacles in Nicaragua, where I had been led into unnecessary danger by inexperienced officers, I had promised my wife I would never again go into combat without at least another American. Also, I wanted to make sure that when I gave the order to fire, there would be at least two rifles fired.

They agreed to that and I returned to New York. I waited and waited, and finally, a week later, they sent me a plane ticket from New York to Martinique, where I was to lay over one night and connect from there to French Guiana. I was to meet Glen in Martinique, and we would proceed together to Cayenne, French Guiana, where we would meet Roy and the two dozen recruits.

When I got to Martinique—where I was supposed to be met with my week-overdue month's pay in U.S. dollars—I was given half a month's pay in Dutch guilders.

When I went to the bank to change the guilders to dollars, I was arrested because the guilders had been stolen, the police informed me.

This did not make me happy, because French jails are unpleasant places. So in answer to their inquiries, I told them where I had gotten the guilders. They arrested Glen. We were held for a few hours—long enough for us to miss our plane— and released. We were either being warned by the French that they were onto us or there really had been a robbery and the Council had somehow been the recipient of the stolen money. Either way, the life of a mercenary suddenly appeared less glamorous than I'd anticipated.

This delay required a few more days of layingover, until the next Air France flight to Cayenne. While we waited in beautiful Martinique I began to inquire of Glen about the makeup of the Council and the general nature of the Surinamese population, both in the country and in exile in Holland. I learned that there were 150,000 Surinamese living in Holland, most of whom went to live there before the Communist revolution. They were economic refugees, I mused, like our government has labeled the Haitians who come here to America. Most of the Surinamese took Dutch citizenship, which they were able to do as former colonial residents, and most of them were on welfare, which is quite high in Holland.

A great concern of these Council members was not to jeopardize their welfare checks.

The Council was tolerated in Holland as long as it didn't do anything bellicose. Members had been told that they would lose their welfare benefits and possibly be kicked out of Holland if anything happened in the way of military ventures against Bouterse. Well, this didn't sound like the kind of motivation that I was used to in Nicaragua, especially with the Miskito Indian refugees. I couldn't imagine anyone telling those boys not to fight to regain their homeland.

But Surinam is not Nicaragua. Nicaragua has a history of violence and passion, and Surinam is kind of an artificial country. Most of the indigenous people were killed, of course, and successive waves of slaves, masters, and laborers have contributed to the present-day population—a combination of Spanish, English, Negro, Hindustani, Javanese, Sumatran, Chinese, Korean, and Dutch.

Spain originally colonized the country, but lost it to England during one of their many wars. The English threw it in to sweeten the deal when they acquired New Amsterdam, now known as New York City, from the Dutch in the seventeenth century. The Dutch governed Surinam until 1975, when they granted full independence to the tiny country on the northeast shoulder of South America. Now it was a Marxist enclave.

Finally we arrived at Rochambeau International Airport, east of Cayenne. There we were met by a couple of Surinamese, a former policeman, and another fellow who described himself as a hustler. He elaborated that he sold heroin and pimped out of a bar that he owned in Amsterdam. Of course the idea of someone giving up a lucrative career like pushing and pimping and tending bar to come fight for his country impressed me greatly. What moral character!

After our arrival I learned that there were no longer two dozen Surinamese recruits. There were now ten. The others got tired of waiting for anything to happen and went back to Amsterdam and welfare. And there was no camp.

The weapons I was promised proved to be two single-shot shotguns, a 16- and a 12-gauge, two .22s, a pistol, and a sawed-off rifle. Not an auspicious beginning for a successful counterrevolution.

CHAPTER TWENTY

BACK TO BASICS

One of the Surinamese expatriates gave us a farm he owned to use as a training camp. It was located some twenty kilometers west of the capital, on the road to St. Laurent and the river border with Surinam. The main building was in poor repair, but there was potable water and ample room for our purposes. Because of the fruit trees everywhere, we christened HQ "Fort Mango."

The first night was spent listening to grown men giggle and tell stories until dawn, just like seventeen-year-old recruits at Fort Jackson.

At six o'clock in the morning I fell out in full fatigues and web gear. Reveille was three shots from my old .45. Two of the recruits, including the former policeman, came out of the house with their hands in the air, thinking that Bouterse's secret police were raiding the camp. I let them know that they were no longer pimps, drug dealers, and welfare chiselers, and that if they wanted to take their country back, they were going to

behave like soldiers and I was going to teach
them how soldiers behaved.

"This man will lead us to hell and back," Giap,
the former pimp, announced to one and all.

Roy showed up a few days later, and together
we arranged a training environment. He also set
up a network of espionage agents that was soon
supplying us with good, cross-verified intelligence
from inside Surinam. Later we learned that, due
to a leak in the Council, Bouterse knew that I
was in French Guiana, and that the resulting
scare had members of the People's Militia wearing civilian clothing under their uniforms so they
could blend into the population quickly when we
attacked.

The recruits were enthusiastic. Only eight of
them lasted out the first few days, but all were
eager to learn how to fight. They wanted their
country back.

Unfortunately their enthusiasm was not
equaled by logistical support from the Council.
Money was always late, short, and in the wrong
currency, so more money would be lost at the
exchange. By the time the other American got
down, weeks after he had been promised, I did
have his money waiting for him in American dollars—a major coup.

Supplies of any kind simply did not exist. We
hunted, foraged, scrounged, and even raided a
few gardens. Hunting trips added such exotic
critters to our diet as anteater, boa constrictor,
anaconda, flamingo, and iguana. Surinamese like
spicy food. Their cooking would make a Mexican

beg for mercy. There must be a stronger word than *hot* for whatever Surinamese food is. I loved it.

The other American's code name was "the Boss." His buddies in basic training had called him that since he was from New Jersey, and they assumed anyone from New Jersey must be a gangster and, therefore, deserving of such a nickname. He was a Vietnam veteran of the 101st Airborne Division's Long Range Reconnaissance Patrols, and just about as crazy as you would expect an LRRP trooper to be. Those guys used to go out in the bush for thirty days at a time, living like the Vietcong. Some of them were scary, but all LRRPs were good soldiers. The Boss had been recommended to me by a Special Forces friend, and one of the best moves that I made on the whole operation was having this fellow come along.

He had gone to Vietnam as a typical nineteen-year-old trooper—the kind we used to refer to as "young, dumb, and full of cum." He came back older, sadder, and confused. He spent two years on the road, sleeping in abandoned cars, drinking from puddles and eating from garbage cans. His only companions on this road back from the organized insanity called the U.S. Army were the ghosts of dead buddies. They used to keep him awake nights asking him what it was all about and why were they dead. He had finally rejoined our world. I was glad for the company and the skills he brought with him.

Finally, the Council succeeded in raising some

money, and Romeo, their able administrator, showed up with some twenty thousand dollars. We journeyed to a country where arms could be purchased with few questions asked and spent the Council's money in one day. Romeo dutifully recorded every purchase in a ledger. We not only bought rifles and ammunition, but uniforms, web gear, packs, bayonets, compasses, boots, and hats. I had an Armalite AR-18 with a telescopic sight for myself, a custom-made XM-16 for the Boss, and American-made Mini-14 assault rifles for the other men.

Romeo returned to Amsterdam to make his report and balance the Council's books. I radioed Roy to inform him of our successful shopping trip. In reply he was to inform me via a coded message whether I was to return via Air France into Rochambeau or if I should seek out some Brazilian smugglers we had made contact with and bring the almost half ton of arms, ammo, and other military equipment into French Guiana in their boat.

The message decoded to read "Rochambeau." That meant that Lautrec, Roy's French Secret Service contact, had arranged for me to sail through customs. I booked a connecting flight to French Guiana, packed the gear in olive-drab duffel bags, and proceeded to the airport. I had to pay another full fare for the extra weight, and almost caused a strike among the baggage workers when they tried to lift the heavy gear. It took considerable greasing of several palms with Council money to calm everyone down and finally get safely out of that country.

Over twelve hours later I landed at Rochambeau, having survived another scar when the bags were transferred to the Air France plane. I tried to appear calm as I sat by yet another airport window, sipping on the ubiquitous tropical rum drink, and saw two of the duffel bags fall from a baggage cart. Fortunately, the Latino who picked them up and hoisted them back on the stack must have taken their weight as a challenge rather than a cause for suspicion. He threw them back up on the cart, said something to a companion with a laugh, and hauled them from the plane I'd arrived on to the nearby Air France jet. I breathed easier and ordered another drink.

I loaded the seven bags on a pushcart and headed to the "Nothing to Declare" line at customs. Thinking the man on duty was in on Lautrec's deal with us, I pushed the heavily laden cart past the bemused gendarme and into the main terminal, where three of my men waited. They threw me and the bags into a waiting truck and raced toward Fort Mango.

"What's the rush, fellows?" I asked

When he stopped giggling Giap told me that Lautrec had called an hour before—his man would not be on duty that night.

"All's well that ends well," I said, rolling my eyes in the direction of whatever deity had been looking out for me. But I was wondering, at the same time, what the penalty might be for arms smuggling in France.

When we returned to the camp I called a general formation and distributed the new U.S. Army jungle uniforms, pistol belts, load-bearing harnesses, rucksacks, bayonets, compasses, boots, two pairs of socks, bush hats, and camouflage makeup to each man. Then, with Roy logging in serial numbers, the Surinamese patriots filed by, one at a time, and received a brand-new rifle and two hundred rounds of ammunition. The men were overjoyed.

Maybe we were going to war after all. After three weeks of intensive night and day training, four of the eight were as close to combat-ready as they were ever going to get, given that they were all over thirty years of age and, with only a few exceptions, had not led lives that included physical exertion.

Meanwhile, I had made a reconnaissance into Surinam. There I was—dugout canoe, piranha-infested river, broiling sun over the malarial jungle, stinging plants and biting insects—armed, dangerous, and alone. I scouted the town of Albina, right on the border across the Maroni River from St. Laurent du Maroni. I felt like I could have taken the town with my .45.

It was Sunday afternoon—four military police at the port of entry and fifty off-duty soldiers. I shot two rolls of film—landing sites and targets—and made my way back.

Shortly after my armed incursion into Surinam, a couple of our spies were caught. Security was tightened all along the border, but not to any degree that would have hampered an operation against Albina. I had three plans for attacks from Fort Mango. All three were canceled at the last minute by the Council for the flimsiest of reasons.

All along, of course, we had help from the French Secret Service. You don't do too much in their territory without them knowing about it. They entered the scene primarily as a result of their attempts to recruit Roy. He was a prize for any intelligence agency—handsome, urbane, and multilingual, he could pass for a member of almost any race or nationality. Even the CIA had tried to recruit him after the Bouterse revolution. Roy, on orders from the Dutch, played the Americans and the French along, never really committing himself but keeping them interested.

The French wanted to use Roy to infiltrate Action Directe, the violent independence movement that had been responsible for several bombings against government offices in France itself as well as their overseas departments.

When the Secret Service learned that an American was running an operation on French soil, they prevailed on Roy for an introduction. We met three of their agents in a small town south and east of Cayenne. The agent in charge was our old friend Lautrec, and he said he was going to help us in our mission. Lautrec explained that the French did not appreciate a Marxist government next door to their Arienne rocket base, and that even if they hadn't been ordered to help us, the Secret Service would do it anyway.

He told us that our camp was under surveillance by the prefecture of police and that we would have to move. We got into a dugout canoe, powered by a small outboard, and set off through the maze of rivers and mangrove, searching for a new site for our camp. When Roy and I complained that this area was too far from the border, Lautrec told us not to worry.

"We run the sky-diving clubs in French Guiana," he said, raising his hand palm-upward and fingers pointed down in the universal symbol of a descending parachute. "We will provide an aircraft and parachutes and drop you into Nickerie. The farther away from French territory, the better for our government."

Lautrec continued, "We can load you up at Rochambeau International Airport after the last Air France flight on any evening. If you need more help, we might even send a few Foreign Legionnaires in with you, if you can pay them."

"Hell," one of his companions laughed, "pay them enough and they'll probably desert and stay with you." He punctuated this declaration with a Gallic flourish of his arms.

This is getting better and better, I thought. *My life is like a fucking 1950s black-and-white foreign-intrigue film.*

We didn't find a suitable campsite that day. We parted with a promise from Lautrec that he would continue the search for us and contact us when they had found a place. He added that he would try to keep the gendarmerie off our backs, but that he couldn't promise anything.

One of the other things that Lautrec did for us was arrange a meeting between Dr. Chin-A-Sen and a cabinet-level minister of the French government. Later I was told that Chin-A-Sen had not handled himself well. He had presented a list of demands rather than establishing rapport. Also, they said that the Communist members of the French Cabinet found out about our presence in French Guiana and demanded our expulsion.

At this time we had eight troops, two Americans, and one politician at Fort Mango. We had put them through a training cycle that involved physical training, obstacle courses, radio procedure, marksmanship, and the care and cleaning of small arms—which is all we ever had—no mortars, no machine guns, no grenades, no plastic explosives, nothing heavy. We had done a lot of ambush and counterambush practice, night field problems, long hikes through jungle and swamp, crossing rivers and crossing major highways during the day. The men had all met my training requirements.

We hadn't heard from Lautrec in over a week, so we decided to take the four best men inside, raid and either retreat into French Guiana or coordinate with reinforcements, led by Roy, in an attack on Albina. At the last minute the Fat Man financed a half dozen more warm bodies. They were all either veterans or had been trained by the Belgian mercenary. I had little time to train them, but they knew what they were doing. They responded well to an accelerated schedule, with Roy in charge.

We were going to leave the new fellows with Roy to finish their training while the Boss, the four commandos, and I went in. We would either meet them at Albina and coordinate an attack there or infiltrate back into French Guiana.

This was also postponed by Council order.

The Boss and I were wondering if these people really wanted a war. We knew some spies had been captured. We knew Roy was working for the Dutch. We wondered about the Council's concern with keeping their welfare checks.

To draw the line—and to vent our frustration —we offered to go in alone. The two of us would start their goddamned war for them. This gesture was also refused.

Our offer wasn't quite mad. Based on my intelligence estimate, and some good leaks from American journalists and the U.S. Embassy in Paramaribo, I figured the Surinamese Army could be taken prisoner by a company of U.S. Marines or the equivalent. Two ex-paratroopers would probably have put a hell of a scare into them at the very least.

But the Council didn't want the Surinamese Army taken by any means. They were interested in publicity and the money drawn by publicity. The Council tried to pick my media contacts because they wanted the word out that they were fighting to liberate their country, even if it wasn't true. Naturally, I wasn't very happy with this. I was hardly prepared to wire *Paris Match* our plans for an invasion of Surinam from French territory. Still, they tried to persuade me to arrange publicity for them.

Press might have done us some good if we

could have gotten some coverage inside Surinam. That way support might have rallied and the bad guys might have been frightened. But the dictator Bouterse controls the press completely. If he chose to ignore us, we could actually invade Surinam, and most of the Surinamese would never know the difference. I decided to compromise.

At the insistence of the Council I dusted off my Cable News Network contacts. I had met some of their boys in Nicaragua when I was fighting for Pastora. Chuck DiCaro and his cameraman, Ken Kelsch, a Special Forces Vietnam veteran, never had gotten an interview with me, but they had voiced an interest in newsworthy anti-Communist activities. I sent them a message saying they would find news if they came my way. If they didn't, NBC would be glad to do so.

CNN came right down.

First they went to Surinam to interview the dictator. That didn't pan out because of Bouterse's paranoia concerning Americans, but they got good footage showing the repressive nature of the regime, although some of it was staged. Kelsch told me they had bribed two Surinamese soldiers to search their rental car while he shot the episode with a hidden camera. They filmed in our camp for a couple of days. Ken had been a recon officer in Vietnam, and even he was impressed with our troops. The soldiers wanted to learn, and the Boss and I felt that we had done our job.

Release of the film report was supposed to coincide with our attack. Actually, CNN wanted to come in and film the assault, but I refused permission. It was going to be bad enough crawling, running, and shooting in the green hell without video equipment and journalists to worry about, although I had no doubts about the courage of either Kelsch or DiCaro. I couldn't guarantee their safe return, so I sent them on their way.

They went back to the States to await our invasion of Surinam. However, on a Thursday night we learned from Lautrec that the French police were going to raid us, close the camp, kick us all out of the country, and possibly press weapons-trafficking charges. We were also told that if the gendarmerie was afraid to go after us, the Foreign Legion—twenty kilometers away at Kourou—had been placed on alert.

That cinched it. French politics may vacillate, and French bureaucrats may give you a break here, or break you there, but if the Legion gets into the act, your days of uncertainty are over. I had no desire to fight the Foreign Legion at all, nor did I have any desire to go to a French jail again.

I demanded expense money for the Boss and myself and told Glen that we would check into a hotel and wait to hear from them. They could wait until this blew over, or until things got patched up in Europe, or until Hell froze over. We would wait until Monday.

On Monday, Lautrec and another agent showed up at our hotel and told me that Saturday, March 24, 1984, the camp had been raided. Everyone had been deported to the Dutch dependency of Curaçao, since most of them had Dutch passports. They were going to be sent back to Holland.

"We must continue our relationship," Lautrec told me. "But I must have another code name, since this operation is now over."

He extracted a small card from his wallet and wrote a number on it. "Call me if you get any assignments that might have an effect on French interests," he said. "Ask for—"

"You were 'Lautrec' for this operation," his companion interjected. "How about 'Toulouse' for the next one?"

Gallic wit. I loved it.

These fine Frenchmen protected us from the gendarmes, and on Monday, March 26, shipped us out of the country. The Boss was to fly from Cayenne to Martinique to Paris to Amsterdam, where the Council said they would have his ticket to America waiting for him. My ticket took me to Martinique, connecting a few days later to New York. There are worse places in the world to have a forced layover during March.

We left on the same plane. The Boss stayed on the 747 for Paris, and I got off in Martinique.

I was met by gendarmes with metal detectors.

"Anything to declare, M'sieu?" the huge, black customs officer queried, his right eyebrow arched quizzically.

"Nothing," I responded.

"*Nothing*, M'sieu?" The eyebrow climbed higher.

"Nothing," I said, with a conviction I didn't feel.

The eyebrow had now merged with his hairline as he listened to my denials.

The metal detectors screamed when they passed them over my duffel bag.

"Come with me, M'sieu." The customs officer directed me to a back room where my bag was opened and searched. When the gendarmes gleefully began adding up charges a couple of Europeans—secret service agents, I surmised—walked in and dismissed the uniformed policemen with a wave of the hand.

"Now, M'sieu," one of them said, "you will check your weapons while you are in Martinique. They will be returned when you leave. I have been instructed to tell you that while we like what you do, you may no longer do it in French territory."

"By the way, M'sieu," the other European asked, "just what is it that you do?"

All former parachutists, these Frenchmen were helpful, polite, and outspokenly anti-Communist and pro-Ronald Reagan. I could not speak too highly of them. They visited while I waited in relative luxury at the Hotel Meridien two days before connecting with my flight to New York.

The logistics of our operation were a mystery to them. Since the operation was blown, I shared this piece of information and received great appreciation for my candor. After business was done it was Kronenbourg time at a local bistro.

CHAPTER TWENTY-ONE

BACK TO THE BUSH

I returned to New York and went to work, trying to salvage what remained of my marriage to the lovely Alexandra Natasha Tarasova and the rest of my life. My mercenary expedition to South America had ended in failure, albeit through no fault of my own. The war in Nicaragua was going badly—the Democratic Alliance in the south was a shambles after the Pastora faction left. Congress had cut off all aid to the Contras and the FDN was carrying on the war as best they could with contributions from American and Latin businessmen. It seemed that my search for a new career had resulted in a dead end, and Alexandra was less than happy about me risking my life all over the world with little or nothing to show for it.

But I was in New York and New York is the business capital of the world. If there's anything businesses use nowadays, it's computers and people who know how to use them. Having been a programmer for several years, I read up on some of the microcomputer innovations and started free-lancing for some of the *Fortune* 500 firms, designing computer systems for their special projects. It was lucrative, and within a few months Alexandra and I were together in a comfortable Staten Island apartment overlooking the harbor. I can't say that I was bored, but it was hard to get too excited over new hardware and software products after having worked on the rise and fall of governments and having dealt with death on a daily basis.

I kept up with the news of the conflict in Nicaragua. Pastora had finally taken a town . . . after a fashion. The civilian population of San Juan Del Norte had been evacuated by the Sandinistas in 1983. But Pastora attacked the sixty-five defenders with a force of over four hundred Contras. After four days of bloody fighting they finally prevailed and captured the town and all sixty-five members of the EPS garrison. Several Contras had died in the battle, but not one Sandinista. Pastora immediately held a press conference and failed to attend to consolidating his modest gain. The Sandinistas launched an immediate and fierce counterattack and retook the town in less than four hours. When queried about his failure to hold real estate dearly purchased, Pastora told a newsman that he was not in business to capture territory, that his was a guerrilla war, and, further, that the CIA had forced him into the ill-advised operation against San Juan Del Norte. I wondered how many of my friends had died there.

A few months later a bomb went off at one of Pastora's press conferences, killing two journalists, including an American—the daughter of the publisher of the *Tico Times*—and costing Popo Chamorro his left eye. The CIA and the Sandinistas were the public suspects. My thoughts were that the Nicaraguan patriots had finally had enough of Pastora and his poor leadership.

In the late spring of 1985 I noticed a small article almost buried in the back pages of the newspaper. It seemed that Alfonso Robelo, of the former Democratic Alliance, along with Adolfo Calero and Arturo Cruz, of the FDN, had signed a pact uniting their efforts to overthrow the Sandinistas.

Their new organization was called "UNO." The acronym stood for Union of Nicaraguan Opposition. *Uno* is also the number "one" in Spanish. I appreciated the symbolism.

I felt a quiver of excitement; my mind raced. With the north and south united militarily, it could be a whole new war. And with almost the entire body politic of the Nicaraguan exiles finally united, the fratricidal bickering might stop and a political and diplomatic offensive could be launched to gain world support for their cause. The U.S. Congress might even be persuaded to resume aid.

I knew that I was going back . . . sooner or later.

Actually, it was easier than I thought. A few phone calls to old contacts in Miami and Los Angeles, a trip to South Florida and a meeting with

El Negro, and I was on my way, once again a member of an armed group fighting the Sandinista government of Nicaragua.

The hardest part of extracting myself from civilian life had been getting clearance. No, not from the CIA or any of the other initialed agencies, but from my wife.

I decided humor was the best way to approach her.

"I'll be damned! Look at this," I said, pointing to an article in *The New York Times*. "There's still injustice and suffering in Central America. I've got to go, Alex. Help me pack my duffel bag."

She looked at me with practiced patience and asked with resignation in her voice, "Do you mean to tell me you're going to walk out on more than forty thousand dollars a year on Wall Street and go live in the jungle again?"

I should have waited till after breakfast. She had the coffeepot in her hand. *I better come up with something good,* I thought.

"Look," I told her, "in a way, it's better now. I've talked to Don Francisco, Robelo's agent in Miami, and Pastora is out. Negro Chamorro is commander of the democratic forces now. And you know I've always gotten along with him and his people. They've asked me to come back, Alex, to set up a training program. Wall Street will be here when I get back."

After extracting a blood oath that I would return by September, she helped me pack my uniforms and gear.

Before going into Central America you really

need a program to describe the teams as well as the players. I mused on the flight south, going over the situation in my mind.

In the north, still operating out of camps along the Honduran–Nicaraguan border, was the FDN, Fuerzas Democraticas Nicaragüense. This was an outfit set up by the Central Intelligence Agency that had received its major funding from our government. Politically, they ranged from middle of the road to ultraright and there was a heavy influence of former Somocistas, followers of deposed and departed General Anastasio Somoza.

Also in the north was the Misura organization, composed of Miskito, Suma, and Rama Indians. Misura, I had been told, had been penetrated by the Cuban DGI and its effectiveness as a fighting force severely compromised. Two CIA case officers either lost their jobs or were transferred to the American equivalent of Siberia over their failure to detect and foil the DGI operation.

On the southern Atlantic coast was Miurasata, the Sandinista-oriented Indian group, led by Brooklyn Rivera. Rivera had been holding talks with the government in Managua and few, if any, of his fighters were operating on the southern front. Spadafora, the former commander of Rivera's forces, had returned to his native Panama, where he was being touted as a presidential contender. His mutilated body was found dumped across the Costa Rican border some months later.

Pastora had been active, at least in the newspapers. He still controlled, he claimed, some seven

hundred fighters along the Rio San Juan, although he had lost a great deal of territory,
camps, and lives in the last year or so. Pastora
was, at that time, considered "missing." There
were rumors of a helicopter accident inside Nicaragua. I had it from three different intelligence
sources that Pastora had been considering a return to the Managua government. And in *La
Republica,* a Costa Rican newspaper, Pastora was
quoted as saying that he had not ruled out such a
return. So it was very possible that he might have
suddenly popped up in Managua, once again a
member of the Communist government.

Alfonso Robelo was still the head of the MDN
and had also allied himself with Negro Chamorro.

Fernando "El Negro" Chamorro had been one
of the first Nicaraguan leaders to have rebelled
against the Sandinistas. For years he led FARN,
Fuerzas Armadas Revolucionarias Nicaraguense,
a small but disciplined commando force that operated, at times, deep inside Nicaragua. Chamorro was now the military commander for the
UNO forces in the south. Unlike Pastora, Chamorro was not afraid to fight personally. I looked
forward to serving under his command.

The first thing I learned when I arrived at the
headquarters in San José was that MDN was
poor. When American aid dried up Robelo insti-
tuted a severe austerity program and many of the
exiled group's salaried employees were let go.
This austerity was reflected throughout the entire
political organization and even into the military.

In a way, this was good. When I was with the

democratic alliance, fighters at the front grumbled about the fat salaries some of the administrative personnel were receiving, and I had noticed that the farther from the front a member was, the more likely he was to have new combat boots on his feet. It was not like that anymore. Expenditures were controlled and carefully audited. Books were kept and accountability was the order of the day. At headquarters every staff member wore a minimum of three hats and put in a minimum of ten hours a day.

The poverty was also reflected in logistics, as I learned when I was told that I would have to take a bus up to the base camp. No vehicles were available.

No problem, I thought, and swinging my duffel bag onto my shoulder, I headed to the bus station for a long ride to the frontier. Several of us were on that bus, including Carlos, the Cuban with whom I had ridden to the front two years previously. He was still there, still fighting. Apparently I had been wrong in my suspicions about him.

We arrived at a border town and were met by more MDN members. As always, profuse hospitality, albeit humble, was extended and we were made comfortable for the night. I was quartered in the private home of a collaborator and began to reorient myself to Central America.

The next day a vehicle arrived driven by Pappy, an old comrade in arms from my days with the alliance, M3, and, obliquely, the Surinam caper. Pappy was Nicaraguan, but a veteran of the U.S. Army. He had seen combat service in

the Korean War. His present job was to organize
the base camp and training program as well as
staging areas for operations.

He spoke excellent English as well as his native
Spanish. He briefed me on the political and military events that had transpired since I had seen
him last, eighteen months previously. Many of
my friends were dead.

Ryan, the Vietnam vet and close friend of
mine, had died when the Sandinistas attacked
Camp Tango. They had bombed the place first
and then brought in special forces by helicopter
in a classic pincer's movement. Ryan was on the
radio. He described the battle over the air as they
fought to the last man against the attacking
Sandinistas. Ryan looked around and saw that *he*
was the last man and dived into the Rio San Juan
trying to escape. The weight of his gear took him
to the bottom. Five days later his bloated body
popped to the surface, miles downstream.

Ryan and I had been close. He had looked out
for Alex and helped her learn Central American
customs. He was the one who had christened me
"soldado sin fortuna," soldier without fortune.

I'd been paid in counterfeit French francs,
stolen Dutch guilders, and, occasionally, American greenbacks by the Surinamese and had
fought mostly for free in Nicaragua. And it was
becoming obvious, even to me, that I'd never get
rich fighting on behalf of freedom and democracy. So the *"soldado sin fortuna"* label that Ryan
had given me seemed very appropriate.

My old friend Surdo, who had almost gotten

me killed when we were operating out of Luna Roja, had lost four fingers to a single AK-47 round. He was retired. Tonio and Tadeo, two of Pastora's commanders, had also retired. They had bought ranches in Costa Rica and were living the life of gentlemen farmers. Tadeo also bought a nightclub. The generally accepted explanation for their ability to do this was that they had stolen the money by diverting supplies from their camps into the black market. When I heard this I thought of the weeks at Luna Roja in which we had had nothing to eat but rice and beans.

Other news from Pappy's update was that Pitufo, a twelve-year-old Miskito boy who had fought with us, never made it to his thirteenth birthday. He had joined us on the Rio San Juan after the Sandinistas murdered his parents, an orphan with no family and nowhere to go. Oscar, one of the squad leaders, had taken the boy under his wing and taught him how to soldier and how to exact revenge. Now Pitufo was dead.

Many others were dead, wounded, or had just gone home, tired and disgusted from fighting a war with not much more than their bare hands. This was true with a lot of the administrative and political people also. These were men with families, children, and other pressures and demands. Dr. Taboada, of M3, had gone to a teaching post at a Canadian university. Cesar Aviles had moved to Los Angeles and was in the import-export business. Others had gone to the United States but found that they could not bear life as an exile and had returned to rejoin the struggle, more determined than ever.

Before reporting to Contra headquarters in San José I'd stopped at a few of the bars to see acquaintances and catch up on the expatriate gossip. I also chatted with a few spooks and freelancers. It came as no surprise to learn that my embassy contact had been promoted and transferred. He was now in the Sinai Desert, probably in operations. But the shocker was learning that the Hippie and Angie had quit the business and gotten married! They had returned to the States, where she was doing some postdoctoral work at Ohio State University.

When we arrived at the base camp, just across the border into Nicaragua, I met a half dozen former comrades-in-arms among the fifty guerrillas stationed there. I also met several more who had known my wife when she had worked as a nurse for the Democratic Alliance back in '83. She had been very popular with the wounded men, who were extremely gratified that a gringa cared enough about them to come to Central America and tend to their wounds.

Our first order of business at this camp was inventory. First of personnel, second of equipment. Half of the men had combat experience, some as much as eight years of combat experience fighting against Somoza and then against the Sandinistas. There were two Cubans with Angolan military service. They had been on the Mariel boatlift in 1980 and had gone to Central America to fight against the Castro-supported Sandinistas.

In all, the men were healthy, physically fit, and their morale was extremely high.

Equipment, however, was another story. FDN had recently purchased five thousand German-made G3 assault rifles, 150 of which were dropped to El Negro's forces, twenty-five at this camp and 125 at another farther into enemy territory. We had one Browning automatic rifle of War World II vintage, two Soviet-made RPK light machine guns, and an assortment of Aks, FALs, and a few civilian-version semiautomatic 5.56-mm assault rifles. We had an RPG-7 with a couple of dozen rockets, ammunition for the M79 grenade launcher, and .50-caliber machine-gun ammo. Unfortunately we had no M79 grenade launcher or .50-caliber machine gun.

There were two 60-mm mortars with crews that had been trained by an ex-Marine captain, then executive editor of *Soldier of Fortune* magazine, Dale A. Dye, who had visited the region and volunteered his services for a time. Later he gained a measure of fame as technical adviser and actor in the film *Platoon*.

Communication equipment was straight from Radio Shack. Uniforms and boots consisted almost exclusively of donations from American veterans groups in the States. At least half of the medicine had come from the bathroom cabinets of American veterans who had responded to the Contras' pleas, published in *Soldier of Fortune* magazine. More was needed.

I went back to the States to report on the Contras' needs. A friend of mine had contacts in the

National Security Agency and she had agreed to act as a cutout between them and me. However, the response to her initial inquiry didn't come from the NSA. Another agency, apparently CIA, contacted her and told her that they would be the recipient of anything I had to report. They referred to me by name, even though she hadn't mentioned who I was when she had tried to contact NSA. I passed on the inventory of men and equipment, together with a list of needs, and after meetings with supporters in New Jersey, Washington, and Miami, I returned to the capital city of Costa Rica.

From there it was another bus ride to Upala, a frontier city teeming with our sympathizers and more than a few Sandinista agents. The bus wasn't quite one of the "pig and chicken specials" that career around precipitous mountain curves in many South American countries but it was close. Filled mainly with *campesinos* from the border area returning from shopping excursions into the big city, it went north for about a hundred kilometers on the Pan-American Highway, then turned off onto a side road that rapidly deteriorated into the usual set of ruts. A few hours of this and I was back at the frontier town of Upala.

I hoisted my duffel bag onto my shoulder and walked the block and a half to the organization's safe house. There I was greeted by the *duena* and her giggling daughters, who brought me a steaming plate of rice, beans, and *bistec*. As I shoveled in the substantial fare I couldn't help notice the flashing dark eyes and giggles of the daughter who was serving me.

"*Quantos anos tiene?*" I asked. "How old are you?"

"*Catorce,*" she giggled.

I snorted and smiled ruefully as I returned to my rice and beans.

Fourteen is a bit too young, I mused. Even for me.

The next morning Pappy showed up with a jeep full of supplies and told me we were going back to Camp Cero Siete, which I'd left only a week previously.

I threw my gear into the back of the jeep and we bounced out of the frontier town and onto the road (of sorts) that would take us to a point about halfway to the camp. From there we would proceed the rest of the way on horseback. As we bounced along the track Pappy told me that Cero Siete had been hit hard during my absence. The camp commander had not followed my advice and had failed to establish patrols to control the region beyond his perimeter. The Sandinistas had crept right up to the camp, mined almost all the access trails, and set up ambushes within shouting distance of the camp. We lost five killed and four wounded to the mines and the ambushes.

Then the Sandinistas got cocky and actually had the nerve to launch an attack against Cero Siete shortly after my return. They infiltrated at least five hundred meters deep into the "neutral territory" of Costa Rica with a platoon that struck from the rear simultaneously with a frontal attack against Cero Siete's main camp. The attack was preceded by a mortar barrage but was beaten off easily by our men's rapid response. We took no casualties during this defense, and judging from the odors that emanated from the jungle over the next several days, we had killed more than a few of them.

Before catching the bus to the frontier I had had a meeting with the *Commandante-en-jefe*, Negro Chamorro. He had requested that I inspect the defensive positions at the various camps and advise the commanders on strengthening these positions. I was to then set up a training center in a secure area and start processing recruits. While we drove Pappy and I discussed the layout of the twin camps at Cero Siete and tried to think of all the possible Sandinista assault routes and how to best defend our position with our thirty-nine remaining troops.

After an hour or so of laboring along muddy trail, we arrived at the *finca* of a collaborator. Charol, commander of the zone, was waiting for me with two horses. I changed from civilian clothes into a new set of jungle-weight camouflage fatigues, threw my gear across the saddle, and mounted up. Pappy returned to Upala with two men who had come down with malaria. Remembering my experience two years previously, I felt for them.

The horses picked their way through the mud and Charol and I discussed the casualties Cero Siete had suffered during my absence.

"Bionica was the first to get it," Charol told me.

Bionica was a seventeen-year-old girl. A Costa Rican whose father was Nicaraguan, she had volunteered to serve in the forces of El Negro. Usually I do not like the idea of women in a combat zone. They cause problems between the men, they usually lack the endurance to be of much value on missions, and in my experience have functioned marginally but adequately only as sentries.

Bionica, however, was an exception. Besides being pretty, she was cheerful and industrious and a real soldier. She could make an AK-47 chatter and, not only that, most of her bullets would end up in the same general area. She took her turn cooking at the main camp, and would even wash the clothes of those too lazy to do their own laundry.

She stepped on a mine. When she fell several others in the patrol, including her boyfriend, rushed out to recover her body and they stepped on more mines. One of the Costa Rican volunteers had quit on the spot when Bionica's severed arm had flown through the air and smacked him in the face.

The Sandinistas had put "Bouncing Bettys" in the center of the trail. These fiendish devices were first developed by the Germans during their preparation for World War II. When activated by pressure, a charge propels the main canister up and out of the ground to a height of about four feet, where it then explodes and sends pieces of shrapnel in all directions. They had also placed even more powerful antipersonnel mines along the sides of the trail. These larger mines could be detonated not only by pressure but by trip wires, and when some of our people dived to the side of the trail in response to the blasts, they had set off even more mines. The effect was disastrous.

"Tatarate got it also," Charol continued.

Tatarate had been a basic-training instructor and I had had my eye on him from the start as a potential instructor when we opened our formal training center. A burly, muscular man, he was gentle and soft-spoken. A good person. I felt his loss and still feel it now.

Charol went on. Daniel had lost a finger to an AK-47 round, the second person I've known to suffer such an amputation. Manuelito, a devil-may-care Cuban, was in a hospital in San José, minus two feet of intestines. He had literally held himself together for eight hours while he was evacuated, on foot, by horseback, and, finally, by jeep to a hospital.

The news was depressing. Casualty statistics usually are—especially when you've lived and joked and laughed with those who are now dead and wounded.

The Sandinistas wasted no time in welcoming me back. Maybe, thanks to their spies along the frontier, they really did know I was there. Zorro had told me that Commandante Mario Miranda, commanding officer of the Sandinista garrison at nearby Papaturro, had received my photograph from Managua with orders to kill or capture me.

Johnny Ringo, Zorro, and a few of the other fellows were hanging out in front of the headquarters building after supper one evening. We were shooting the breeze and I was, little by little, beginning to grasp enough of the language, as spoken by Nicaraguan peasants, to be able to converse casually, like we were doing. I had just taken a bath from a bucket behind the building and put on a clean set of fatigues. My web gear, containing my grenades and spare magazines, was inside the building, hung on a nail by my hammock. I was sitting on the steps, lacing my boots and enjoying the feel of clean socks, with my G3 rifle across my knees.

I heard the snarling crackle of AK-47s. God, if I could bottle that sound, I could make a fortune selling it as anticonstipation medicine. We could hear an answering burst from a G3 as our sentry by a little river that ran between the two camps of Cero Siete returned the Sandinistas' AK-47 fire. I had rolled across the ground and taken up a position behind the porch and was looking for a target when I saw a green streak flash by and disappear into the building.

Who's that dumb bastard? I thought.

The building was also the armory, and anyone in there, if the building took a mortar or an RPG-7 round, would be history. The green streak emerged and flew by my position. I heard a thump and looked in the direction of the sound. I saw my web gear lying beside me.

As he ran to his position Johnny Ringo shouted

over his shoulder, "You might need the extra
magazines and hand grenades, Dr. John."

This is called "bravery under fire" in any army.
Unselfish, thoughtful, heroic, and a host of other
adjectives came to my mind as I marveled over
the fact that my buddy had just raced into a
prime target for the sole purpose of retrieving my
extra ammunition.

Later that night the enemy probed our defenses again. The Sandinistas were taking a page
from my book. I had talked to El Negro and his
operations staff about initiating night patrols for
the purpose of harassing the enemy and ruining
their sleep for a few nights. The idea was to hit
them with a minimal force, drop a few mortar
rounds into their camp, and withdraw. It's hard
to go back to sleep after you've been awakened
like that. Then, at the crack of dawn after the
third night of such attacks, I wanted to hit them
with a major assault.

The plan had been well received, however, due
to the current Sandinista offensive Commander
Chamorro had suspended our offensive activities
in order to focus maximum efforts toward
strengthening our defenses.

So there was no sleep that night for us, or the
next day.

I went to the main camp to take some photographs of the dispensary that a Panamanian para-
medic had set up. The Panamanian had lived in
Houston, Texas, for a few years and spoke some
English. He was on loan to us from the FDN

forces and had brought some sorely needed medical supplies with him.

When I got to the main camp I found a patrol forming and decided to join it. The mission of the patrol was to detect and recover Sandinista mines, then replant them to give them a taste of their own medicine. We locked and loaded prior to departing from the safety of our perimeter. We crept single file, ten meters apart, through the thick jungle along a barely discernible game trail. The trails, when cut at all, are cut for short Latins, not tall gringos. I was almost duck walking, my rifle at the ready, when less than a hundred yards from the camp, they opened up on us. I dived for the ground and tried to focus on a target, but all I saw was a blur of green and the pale, scared face of the Contra in front of me until I forced myself to calm down. We sprayed the jungle with 7.62-mm bullets.

Off to the right we heard a thrashing about fifty feet off the trail. I looked at the man in front of me and he looked back at me; both of us made hand signals to the effect of "Are you going out there to finish him off?" We both knew the Sandinista might still be able to pull the pin on a grenade and take a Contra with him, and neither of us wanted to move one inch off that trail. Soon the thrashing stopped; we both breathed a sigh of relief.

After fifteen minutes of silent, still waiting, we crept on, deeper into hostile territory. We rounded a sharp turn in the trail and came face-to-face, actually face-to-what-was-left-of-the-

face, of one of our men who had been missing
since a firefight on this same trail eight days before.

Juan Negro had been on a patrol similar to this
one. He had been walking point, the first man on
the trail, his eyes focused on the ground, searching for the mines that had so recently killed his
friends. He might not even have noticed that he
had just entered a clearing. Two steps into that
clearing he died. Two Sandinistas opened up on
him from ambush positions less than fifteen feet
away. The vicious bursts from the Kalashnikovs
caught him in the chest and stomach, killing him
instantly.

Now, we were back . . . back to claim the
territory and the body of our friend.

A messenger was dispatched to the headquarters of Zone Cero Siete and the call went out that
we needed help from our collaborators. Within an
hour seven farmers had gathered with tools and
lumber to build Juan Negro's coffin and carry it
out to the clearing, where we stood guard.

After checking the body for booby traps his
remains were gently, almost lovingly, placed in
the smooth cedar box and carried back to the
main camp for Christian burial with full military
honors.

A few of us stayed at the clearing to search the
area for mines. We located and dug up seven of
the lethal, Czechoslovakian PPM canisters, along
with some other gear the Sandinistas had left
when they retreated from the area. I spotted a

lumpy shape at the edge of the clearing and approached it with caution.

At first all I could see was the souvenir I'd wanted through three wars. An AK-47 bayonet lay on what looked like a pile of rags. Two steps closer and I saw that it was a body and the rags were the rotted cloth of a Sandinista militia uniform.

He couldn't have been more than seventeen or eighteen years old. Small, almost pitifully thin, in spite of the bloating of the corpse, his hands were raised toward the gaping hole in his throat where, eight days previously, his life had flowed out.

What the fuck am I doing here killing children? I asked myself.

A weight settled over me and I knelt beside the body of my former enemy. *Calm down, John,* I told myself. *Death is part of war and war is what it takes to establish freedom and democracy.*

Am I right? I wondered. *Is this the way it has to be?*

I thought back to history lessons . . . the Greeks had established the first democracy and I vaguely remembered the Athenians having to defend themselves from a military dictatorship in Sparta. There seemed to be a gap in my memory for several centuries, or maybe there was a gap in the history of representative government until the barons surrounded King John at Charter Oak in the thirteenth century and forced him to sign the Magna Carta. After that England had fought a succession of bloody civil wars before the final governmental product that ensured freedom and representation for all was hammered out.

The violence and birth struggles of the French Revolution had resulted in more deaths than Nicaragua would probably ever see. Yet the final product was, no doubt, worth it to their progeny.

And when the Latin American countries threw off the oppressive Spanish yoke, it was done with steel and violence and death. And some of those nations were still struggling to achieve democracy. Even peaceful Costa Rica . . . they paid for their liberation from Spain with the blood of their citizens and then, in the same century, rallied all of Central America to defeat the ambitions of William Walker. As recently as 1949, Don Pepe Figueres led a successful revolution in Costa Rica to forcibly remove a president who refused to leave the office when he lost an election. Don Pepe ordered the bodies left to rot in the streets to teach the citizenry what war was all about; then he disbanded the army, leaving Costa Rica as one of the few nations in the world without a war machine. But the price for such peace was blood.

The colonists of our own country had tried every means known to them—politics, diplomacy, appeals in the press, and even tax revolt—before they picked up their guns and gave us the greatest democracy in the history of the world.

But all the history lessons in the world wouldn't bring back Juan Negro or the dead Nicaraguan child before me. But maybe . . . maybe the joys of the democracy I hope and pray is coming to this troubled nation will make the memory of their deaths a little less bitter.

I rose to leave. It was dark in the jungle clearing. It was peaceful.

And I was alone.